YOU DON'T NEED A SYSTEM
A Straightforward Guide to Using the Law of Attraction

Also by Rolf Nabb:

Why Can't I Just Be Happy? A Realistic Approach to Happiness

Dating Sense: The Practical Way to Meet, Date and Marry the Right Person

YOU DON'T NEED A SYSTEM
A Straightforward Guide to Using the Law of Attraction

ROLF NABB

ARTRUM MEDIA

For the L and L'er E's

*Disclaimer: This book is not intended to replace medical advice or be a
substitute for a psychologist. The author and the publisher expressly
disclaim responsibility for any adverse affects of this book. Neither author
nor publisher is liable for information contained herein.*

CONTENTS

IS THIS LAW OF ATTRACTION THING REAL?

I'm sure that this is the first thing on many people's mind when they read a book on the Law of Attraction. Is the Law of Attraction really real? Or is it just a bunch of mumbo-jumbo? Surely, it's as hokey as it seems, right?

The answer is that yes, it is real. However, if you listen to some of the experts out there, it will really sound like a bunch of mumbo-jumbo. And it will sound extraordinarily hokey. In fact, it will sound so far-fetched that most people will dismiss it without giving it a second thought. That's where this book is different. I will show you how it isn't just a bunch of metaphysical malarkey but rather a basic idea of what you give out, you get back. It's the idea that your attitude is everything and if you have a good one, then good things will happen to you.

I do not claim to know everything there is to know about the Law of Attraction because I don't. No one does. However, I do think I have a very good grasp on the concept and I can explain it in a way that even skeptical people can understand and accept. In fact, many people will even say that this book is not even about the Law of Attraction because it is such a different take on it. However, they would be wrong. The Law of Attraction is not a magical thing. In fact, if you think of all the bromides and parables and fables that you have heard in your life, you should already have the concept. It is so simple that many people miss it. It is not even that hard of a concept to understand but, because of the guru mentality of so many of the experts, it is made so much more difficult than it really is. They have made it sound as though you have to do all sorts of strange things in order to utilize it. They make it sound as though you have to have some sort of system. That you have to follow the teachings of somebody you've never heard of without knowing if their sole motivation is just to get the cash from your wallet. You don't. You just have to approach things in your life differently.

There are also many people out there who preach that you should be very careful of what you do or how you think because if you're not careful, you'll attract something bad even though you have good intentions. If you want more money, you'll continue to want more money. If you want to be good enough to do something, you'll continue to want to be good enough to do something without ever achieving what it is that you want to do. They're completely hung up on the semantics. I think that this is wrong and just a little bit short-sighted and just a little bit too literal-minded.

Your intention counts for something and if you look at the Law of Attraction in the manner in which these so-called experts tell you to, you are ultimately powerless over what happens to you. Sometimes you will have down moments, everyone does, but should this one moment of feeling down completely ruin every good thought you have had? Certainly not.

A good example of the fallacy of this simplistic view of the Law of Attraction is that anything you can do can be turned into something bad if you take the intention out of it. For example, according to this view of the Law of Attraction if you want something, you'll continue to want it. However, if you're spending too much money, won't you also continue spending too much money? Regardless of how much you attract in? I think you see what I mean here. If you look at it this way then you're using the examples they give, but turning it completely on itself. When you can do this with a concept, it's plain to see that it's just not that cut and dried.

Here's an example that hopefully will illustrate my approach to the Law of Attraction. An outstretched hand of friendship usually invites more outstretched hands of friendship. A fist usually invites more fists. This is why you have to present the world and other people the outstretched hand of friendship. In other words, what you put out there is usually what you get back. Sure, it doesn't always happen on an immediate and obvious basis, but overall, the good will outweigh the bad. If you're positive and you have good thoughts, you will attract good things. And if you can get into the habit of it, your life will turn around in many different other ways, too because the good things will snowball. If you're good and good to the world and to people around you, you will have good things happen to you. This will cause you to build momentum and this momentum will continue on and more good things will continue to happen. And so forth. This is what the Law of Attraction is.

Also, unlike many of the experts, I'm not going to tell you that you are going to be rich or you're going to come into windfalls of money. I will not make any such promises because your life is your own. I do not know what you want to attract. If this is what you want, then good for you. It's always good to want to do better by yourself and your loved ones. If you can use the techniques and knowledge I give you to achieve your goals, then wonderful. However, I am not going to guarantee you that you will achieve them. This is ultimately up to you. What I will tell you, however, is that if you can accept what the world has to give you and if you truly know what you want, you will be able to achieve it. This does not only apply to material things but also emotional and spiritual things as well. You will be okay. You just have to accept it and keep a positive attitude.

WHY I WROTE THIS BOOK

I'm sure that many of you who are reading this book are thinking to yourself that this is just another self-help book. That this is yet another thing that you're going to read which isn't going work or even apply to your life. In other words, that this is just another piece of crap that has been designed to make big promises and take your money. Hopefully, you won't find this to be the case and you'll be pleasantly surprised. If you take anything away from it, take the idea that attitude is everything. Especially if it's a good one.

While the focus of this book is primarily going to be on money and wealth—this is because this is the main reason why people are interested in the Law of Attraction—it doesn't mean that the same principles cannot be applied to other areas of your life like romance and happiness. In that way, it can be considered a self-help book of sorts. However, I wouldn't classify it that way. The reason I say this isn't really a self-help book is because this book is not really about helping yourself, but about waking you up. It's about making you realize that you have a limited time on this earth and you need to do what you can to enhance your time here. It's about how you have to realize that there are many more opportunities out there in the world that you even knew existed and the reason you don't know about them is because you don't even really know what you want. While I am not very fond of the term, "bucket list," what I want this book to be is a bucket list of possibilities for your life that have yet to happen. That your life isn't over and that you haven't experienced all life has to offer yet. There are always possibilities.

This idea of how the Law of Attraction works is something that has taken me a long time to figure out. If I can help one person to wake up and see what the world has to offer a person who is ready to accept it, then I have done my job.

Let me explain something about myself. I've always been the sort of person who took self-help books with a grain of salt. I always figured, why bother? They aren't going to tell me anything I don't already know. Sure, some of them help people, but many of them don't. Most of them are written by charlatans who promise you the world and then deliver nothing but an invitation to a workshop where you are even further offered the opportunity to spend even more money to learn the "wisdom" that was left out of the book. And then you leave without knowing any more than you did to begin with other than the fact that you just got ripped off. That's where this book is different. I'm not offering anything other than the knowledge that you can change your life and that good things can happen for you if you can just let them and you can usually do this by just figuring out what you want out of life and improving your attitude.

Even though I have read a lot of self-help books, I just never really found anything that applied to me. This is why I took my self-help in the form of literature and in comedy. These books have helped me through hard times and helped me solve my problems. I have found great comfort in the great works of literature and I still refer to some of them in my times of distress. The only problem in this approach lies in the fact that you can't always stumble into the right book or right comedian when you're down. Sometimes this approach will only make you feel worse about yourself. This is why I'm writing this book. I wanted to write a self-help book for people who are sort of skeptical about self-help but want to feel better and do better in their lives. They're the sort of people who feel that they have, for some reason, found themselves adrift but don't necessarily know how they got in the boat.

You have to realize that no matter what people tell you, it is good to be skeptical. It is good to question things. However, you can't let this skepticism go too far. When you question things too much, you become locked up. For example, a good friend of mine would puzzle over and analyze movies he had seen and books he had read to such an extent that eventually he got to the point that he didn't even know if he even liked what he had seen or read. I would ask him his opinion about something and he would start telling me his analysis which would go on for quite some time. Eventually, I would ask him if he liked it, he would say, "You know, I don't really know." His method of thinking had twisted him up so much that he had lost his gut instinct. He no longer knew what he liked or what he wanted. He was so analytical and skeptical of everthing that he had lost the ability to tell what was good and what wasn't. This happens to so many of us in regards to our lives that we never really accomplish what we want and live lives that we never planned on living. We just don't know what we want or like for ourselves. As a result, we end up working jobs and doing things that we don't really like but we never know it. We just know that we think we should be doing something else, but we just don't know what it is.

I know what it's like to be so skeptical and analytical that you can't accept anything. To think that there is no hope. However, I have found that there is help and hope. You just have to accept it. I'm not going to go into the metaphysical either because I know that that's still a speculative area. However, you just have to believe that there is hope and that it is within reach. No matter how dark the night is, there is still a brighter morning.

When it comes to the idea of being open to changing your approach to life, you can use the example of Benjamin Franklin as an example. In his autobiography, he wrote about how at one point in his life, when he was young, he decided that he would attempt to achieve moral perfection. He developed a system whereby he would devote himself to the virtues he was trying perfect. In fact, he kept a book in which he charted his progress. With this system in place, he didn't think that his goal would be that hard to attain. However, when he began to execute his plan of self-examination, he was surprised to find himself "much fuller of faults" than he had imagined. In fact, he still had quite a bit of work to do. The same thing applies to me and self-help books. I thought I knew it all, but then I realized that when it came to understanding the world, I came up woefully short.

I don't think I'm alone in this.

But why should you listen to me, you ask? Why should you listen to a seemingly cynical person who at one point they thought they knew it all? Well, the answer is simple. I woke up one day and realized that I didn't know it all. I found out that there was so much to learn in the world and most of it was easily within reach.

YOU DON'T NEED A SYSTEM—JUST A BETTER ATTITUDE

One of the biggest problems that I have with many of the Law of Attraction gurus is that they try to tell you that you need a system or that you need to spend lots of money to make it work. Sure, there's nothing wrong with spending money for books and videos on the subject, but when people are told that they have to spend the money on the guru's systems—for information that wasn't included in the book—then something begins to smell fishy.

The fact of the matter is that you don't need any sort of system or sweat lodge or any other mumbo jumbo for the Law of Attraction to work for you. All you have to do is improve your attitude.

Yes, you just have to improve your attitude.

The Law of Attaction is a very simple concept. It's so simple that it's hard to grasp. That is why I want to boil it down to its essence. It's completely about your attitude. When it comes to the Law of Attraction, attitude is everything. Good things happen to people with positive attitudes. Good things happen *for* people with positive attitudes. You don't need anything to practice the Law of Attraction other than yourself. You don't need to go through strange rituals. You don't need to be ritually cleansed or purified. All you need is your brain and yourself. All you have to do is to change your outlook and your perspective. Many times these purifications and cleanses are something, that while well intentioned, are merely devices to pull you from your routine and make you change your perspective. I think that you can do the same thing with a vacation to a place other than one you usually go or something enjoyable like that. As long as you do something that is a little challenging and different, you will still change your perspective. The way I see it, changing the way you view the world and yourself should not be a tortorus experience.

You have to always have a positive outlook and positive things will happen for you. Just think of how you react to a person with a bad attitude. You're put off and you want nothing to do with them, right? This is the way the universe reacts too. If you act like you're miserable and unhappy, you're going to continue to experience miserable and unhappy things.

One problem you have to face with having a better attitude is to overcome any self-esteem issues that you may have. People with a low self-esteem think that everything is about them. Conversely people with an inflated self-esteem think the same way. The difference is that people with a low self-esteem unnecessarily perceive that they are put-upon and the focus of bad attention and negativity because they can't help but see things through their own lowered self-image. On the other hand, people with a high self-esteem think that good things happen to them because they are just so great.

While it's true that good things are not always going to happen to you, sometimes things may take a turn for the worse. This is when you really have to struggle to put a good spin on things. You have to see the bright side until you come out of the hole. The power of having positive attitude is a very real thing and whatever you exhibit to the world is what you will get back. The thing is that when bad things start happening in your life, they have a tendency to snowball if you're not careful. Ths is why I keep saying that whatever is going on in your life can gain momentum. Either good or bad. Sometimes bad events happen beyond your control, but if they initially negatively affect your attitude then you're probably going to find yourself going down a rushing river of more bad things happening. Remember like attracts like and birds of a feather flock together, hence the bad stuff is feeding on itself and producing more bad stuff.

It will be tough, sure, but if you can see the bright side of bad things and act cheerfully, you will eventually be cheerful and things will turn around. You have to fake it until you make it because good things will happen but you have to invite them in first.

I know that sometimes I'm not as positive as I can be and I fall short. When I do this, I usually immediately see things take a downturn. Nobody's perfect, but having a positive attitude is a habit more than anything. Also I know for a fact that most people don't really attract bad things into their life per se, but rather they attract them because of negativity and a bad attitude. I know there are exceptions, but this is true an overwhelming amount of the time.

No matter how easy it is, don't let the bad things that happen in your life drive you to a state of despair or despondency. You must have faith. Always. You must always know that things will work out because they will. This pit of despair is an easy one to slide into and a hard one to crawl back out of. So always keep this in mind when you feel the urge to feel sorry for yourself when things don't go your way. Everybody will be faced with obstacles and some will be so horrible that they defy description. But you have only one life to live. Either you live it happily or you don't. This is up to you and if you know this very important pitfall, you will avoid much of the negativity that can plague people's lives.

So just realize that you don't need a system for the Law of Attraction to work for you. You just need to improve your attitude and raise your self-esteem. You need to look on the bright side and keep a good outlook. What you project will reflect back on you and you don't want your negativity to make your life worse than it has to be.

HOW THE LAW OF ATTRACTION REALLY WORKS

Many people go on about the Law of Attraction and explain how it works in extraordinarily metaphysical and elaborate terms. Most of them are dead right, too. However, even after all this explanation many (in fact most) people are still quite not sure of how exactly it works. They still don't understand it. They think that even though it has been explained to them very thoroughly, it is still out of their grasp and until they do it and achieve some success from it, it will continue to be so. In this regard, it is just like swimming, driving a car with a stick shift or riding a bicycle. Explanations defy the simplicity of the concept.

Regardless of this, it is a very simple concept and to many people, this is the problem. It's just too simple. And when it comes to money and love—which is why many people are interested in the Law of Attraction in the first place—this can be detrimental to your finances and your happiness. This is why I feel the need to simplify it so that almost anybody can understand it.

Basically speaking, the Law of Attraction is primarily about what you focus on. What you put out there into the world is exactly what you will get back. In other words, if you send love out, you'll get love back. If you send hate back, you'll get hate back. Just apply this to everything in your life, including money. It's all about how you perceive things. If you focus on how broke you are, then you'll attract more poverty. However, if you focus on your wealth, then you're going to attract wealth. It's really rather simple. It's all about your mindset. If you're a poor-minded person who is always griping about not having money, then you'll never have enough money. You'll always be poor, regardless of how much money you have. And it's also about expectations. If you expect too little, then this is exactly what you'll get out of life. Too little.

While this is on the surface rather simple, when you delve more deeply, it becomes more complicated. This is where many people get off track. This is because much of what you think has probably been ingrained into you from birth. Just look at your family. Were you brought up thinking that you didn't have enough money? Were your parents always scrambling to pay the bills? When it came to your finances, was it always a case of one step forward, two steps back? I'm sure that if you're honest, you probably still think this way now, even if you don't really have any money worries. In your mind, you're still broke. And because of this, unless you change the way you think, you'll always be broke. And what about love? Were your parents happy? Did they love each other? Did they love you? Or were you always feeling like you were not getting enough attention from them? Whatever negative or positive thing that you took from their relationship with each other and with you, most likely is still with you. As a result, many of the problems or triumphs that you experience today are a direct result of it.

This allows us to touch on another concept that is closely connected with the Law of Attraction that also eludes many people. This is the idea of being thankful. You must always be thankful for what you have. If you're not, then it's kind of like you didn't even get it. You didn't recognize when you had something good and as a result, you in effect, never had it. Maybe you might have noticed it when it was gone, but by then it was too late. This is closely related to the old saying that says that wealth not used might as well not exist. If you're not cognizant enough of what you've been granted to be thankful for it, then you might as well not have received it. In order for the Law of Attraction to work, you have to be thankful for everything. You have to recognize how wonderful it is just to be able to get out of bed in the morning. You should be thankful for your life and your family. For the sun in the sky. When you do this, more good things will come. You will recognize all the goodness around you that you've been granted and as a result you will recognize more. This is because you're not being poor-minded any longer and only focusing on your want, but rather being bountiful-minded and focusing on what you have been given.

Seriously, have you ever noticed how good things always seen to happen to people who have a positive attitude? This is no coincidence. Some cynical people will say that the reason why they're so positive is because good things are happening to them. It would be easy to smile and be happy if everything is always coming up roses for you. To them, I say that they're partially right. These people are positive because good things are happening to them. However, good things are happening to them because they are positive as well. This is a cycle that feeds on itself. They have momentum. The same thing happens to people who are negative, but in reverse. It just feeds itself. This is why you must be positive for the Law of Attraction to work.

How it really works is really quite simple. What you put out there is what you receive back. If you're positive, positive things will happen to you. You will find the good in things and make your life so much easier because you won't be spending your life thinking only about the bad in life. You will recognize what you have and be thankful for it. It is very difficult for most people to only focus on what they have rather than what they don't have, but you have to make an effort. At first, you will probably fail a lot, but you will get better. Each failure will lead you to more success because you will learn from it. This is how it really works. Focusing on what you have and being thankful for it is how you change your mindset. Once you get into a bountiful and abundant way of thinking, you will be ready for all the things that you deserve.

ABOUT ME

Before you get too far into this book, I thought that I would tell you a little more about myself and how I came to understand the Law of Attraction. This might help you to understand just what kind of person I am and why my take on the Law of Attraction might be relevant for people who don't really believe in such concepts.

To make a long story short, I was born into a lower-income family that was so rooted in negativity, it's a wonder that they ever got anything accomplished. My father was a construction worker and my mother worked in a factory. While they were loving parents, they had no ambitions or aspirations and they certainly didn't encourage any in my brother or myself. "Just do the least that you can to get by," was my father's maxim. "Don't do any more than you have to," was another saying of his. A lot of this came from the fact that no one in their families had ever had any drive to do anything except simply get by, but much of it came from low self-esteem. My mother acted as though whereever she went, she had to prove that she had a right to be there, as though she was going to be chased off at any second. She would say, whenever we went anywhere, "Just hold your head up and act like you've got just as much right to be there as anybody else." Now this might seem like good advice, but when you haven't done anything to make you think that you didn't belong there in the first place, the message is the opposite of what she wanted to convey. She was, in essence, telling us that we didn't belong there, but we needed to act like we did. My father, on the other hand, just wouldn't go anywhere.

Why was this? I don't know. It's just the way it was and I accepted it and I grew up exactly like this. In my mind, at least.

However, despite all this, I was a very optimistic person as well as quite imaginative and creative and succeeded in school and went on to college. I did well and graduated with honors. But without any sort of guidance or role models to speak of, I had no game plan or idea what I would do afterwards. My parents and relatives were always very mute on the subject. According to them, you just worked at whatever you could get and hopefully someone would eventually give you a decent job. "Start at the bottom and work your way up," they would say. I accepted this and was ready to do what it took to get ahead. Needless to say, after college, I was unable to find any sort of work that was in the least bit creative or engaging. I bounced around a few jobs before finally descending into manual labor at a factory for a few years. What was most telling about the job was that I wasn't even allowed to use a pencil for the first three months I worked there. And here I had been an honor student in college and on this job using a pencil was more responsibility than the bosses thought the employees could handle. Somehow, I eventually managed to "advance" myself to middle management. I spent seventeen years doing this. Despite my "success," I hated my job and I became just as negative as my parents.

But then, there was hope.

I won't bore you with the particulars, but sparked by boredom with my job I started writing. I started out with comic strips—no money was made—which led me to novels and articles. I really enjoyed it, but didn't expect much from it. It was just an outlet from the dreariness I experienced at work. So I wrote for years for my own benefit and then one day, I figured out a way to make it work. I figured out what it would take to get published and after a long while, I began to start achieving some level of success. Not only in writing, but also in some independent business ventures. It was then that I finally began to come into my own. With this little seed of success, my attitude started improving and soon I was as optimistic as I had been in my younger years. From that, I began to achieve more financial success and from there, my attitude really started to improve and things started getting better and better. When this began to happen it was as if a fog had lifted and after many years in the darkness, I was finally starting to see the light. With this awakening, came more awareness. It was like everything was snowballing for me. A veil had been lifted. I began to see that what my parents had been taught was wrong. I began to use my abilities better and utilize the knowledge I had learned through years of a dead end job to my own advantage. I saw instances in my life where cynical bosses and co-workers had taken advantage of my trust and lack of ambition. I had been a target to so many people who had seen the talent and ability in me that I hadn't been able to see myself. I felt like a fool but I was ready to move on to better things. I was gaining momentum and the odd thing about this is no one other my wife seemed to care. My parents were completely indifferent and actually sometimes seemed to resent me over the fact that my fortunes had improved. Some of my friends even tried to sabotage me. The rest of them sort of pretended that I didn't exist.

As a result of my parents' indifference towards my success, I began to be plagued with the idea of how they had never had any drive or ambition. It bothered me that as I got older and became more aware of how the world worked, I began to realize just how stuck they were in their negativity. I loved them, but they really irritated me too. I just couldn't understand how they could be this way.

It was around this time when I found out about the Law of Attraction.

It was very intriguing to me and I really liked what I was reading. However, from my own personal experience, sometimes it seemed just a little too simplified. I knew from my long hard years that sometimes attraction can occur in different ways than having the wrong thought. I knew that much of the time, bad things happen because of bad decisions and because you have a negative attitude. Also I knew that sometimes bad things happen because you run into bad people. None of the books I read ever seemed to address these simple facts.

I knew from working in all different levels with people, as well as growing up around very negative people, the power of perspective and attitude can have on your life. Sure, you can attract bad things, but most of the time, it's not because you visualize them or think them, it's because you're just setting yourself up for them due to what you're doing with your life.

From my own personal experience, I know that there's light at the end of the tunnel if people just start making good decisions and change their outlook. I know it certainly helped me to do this and if I can help another person, then that is reward enough.

YOU HAVE TO KNOW WHAT YOU WANT

Imagine this scenario:

You're sitting around the house and you have nothing to do. You decide to do a little shopping. You go to the mall, wander around for a few hours, make some purchases and then go home. The next day, you look at the stuff you bought and realize that you didn't really want any of it then you take it all back. In other words, you bought stuff to return.

Why did this happen?

It happened because you didn't really know what you wanted so you went and collected a bunch of things that you thought you might want and then you realized later that you really didn't like them after all.

And why am I bringing this up, you ask?

It's simple. This is what many people do with their lives. They don't really know what they want to do so they just wander around doing various things without ever finding any happiness and then end up unsatisfied. They expect nothing from life and they get nothing from life. If they're lucky they get a paycheck and a warm place to sleep. If they're lucky. The only difference between this and going to the mall is you can't always return your life decisions. If you're lucky you can get some second chances, but since the clock is always ticking, time can run out. This is why it's so important for you to know what you want out of life. If you don't know, you will never get it because you will never know when you have it.

Think about your life in ten years; do you see it being any different than it is now? If you want it to turn in a positive direction, you have to figure out what you want first. Then all sorts of opportunities will become apparent to you. It's not like they just materialize out of thin air, but rather when you truly know what you want, you will then recognize opportunities that you would have overlooked otherwise. Do you want an expensive car? Do you want a bigger house? Do you want happiness? Do you want a better paying job? Do you want a husband? A wife? A job? It doesn't matter. If you can just figure out what you truly want, you can begin to take advantage of all the opportunities that the world and life have to offer.

If you're like a lot of people, you're unsure of what you want and just wander from one thing to the next, you need to ask yourself why it is that you want and expect so little from life. I would be willing to bet that if this is the case, the reason why you're so hesitant to admit to wanting anything is because you're afraid of failure. You're afraid if you admit what you want, then you will be setting yourself up for the disappointment of not getting it. Life has no guarantees, I'll agree with you there. However, if you aren't admitting that you want anything, you are experiencing disapointment without ever giving yourself the chance to attain what it is that you want.

Failure will inevitably happen. This much is true. But you shouldn't look at it as a bad thing because success will happen too and so much of it will happen that you never counted on if you will just give yourself a shot and keep working towards your goals. If you will just dare to dream with the idea that you are always thankful for what you have and that if you aren't quite ready for what you want, you're willing to wait. You should never let a disappointment make you unhappy forever. You need to ask yourself if there is one thing in your life that you've always wanted. The next question is are you going to be unhappy in your life if you don't achieve it? Is it going to make you miserable person or are you going to be able to move on and enjoy your life with other things that can realistically make you happy.

The answers to this should cut you two ways. You need to be happy in yourself without this one thing. However, if there's this one thing that's going to make you happy out there, why aren't you at least admitting to yourself that it exists? Are you just trying to make yourself suffer? It's said that the reason we want things is because we think that they will make us feel better. But if you can't acknowledge what these things are, then how will you ever hope to feel better?

You have to dare to dream. You cannot be complacent. The lives of many great men are filled with many disappointments and failures, but the difference between them and men who remain failures is that they never gave up. They never let anything stop them because they knew what they wanted and they were willing to accept a little failure to get it.

If you're uncertain or conflicted about what you want, make a list. Write all the things you want out of life. At first it may be a little tough because you're going to have trouble admitting that you want anything more than what you have. You'll be scared to find out that you discover what you have a little lacking, but continue on anyway. Do you want a better job? Write it down. Do you want a girlfriend? A boyfriend? Write it down. After you're finished, write this list again. It will be easier this time. Continue this until you can readily admit what you want out of life and if there's part of your life you want to change. After this comes the fun part. You start *concentrating* on what it is you want. You start to think about them in a meaningful way and think about how you can attain them. Not all the time, mind you, but look at your list from time to time and remind yourself. You can revise it if necessary. This is when you start to notice that there are a lot of opportunities out there for you to attain what you want. You will see things that you never thought about before because you never thought you had to. This is when you start getting what you want out of life. This is when you start realizing the incredible power of the Law of Attraction. But for this to happen, you have to complete the simple act of figuring out what exactly it is that you want. When you don't know, the Law of Attraction will only bring in a blah life with limited opportunities. It needs your focus. Without focus, you will live an unfocused life. This is why this is so important.

We'll go more in depth into the individual aspects of what I'm talking about in this chapter throughout this book. We'll explore manifesting, visualization etc…but I wanted to bring it all together in the beginning to show up just how practical and simple the Law of Attraction is. So if you're serious about the Law of Attraction, you need to start evaluting your wants. You cannot be afraid to admit that what you have is lacking and understand that it's okay to want more. You can be thankful for what you have and still want more. But first you just have to figure out what you want. Because, seriously, if you don't know what's going to make you happy, who does?

THE MEANING OF MONEY

In the words of the great writer, Henry Miller, "And then no money, or a little money, or less money, or more money but money always money and if you have money , or you don't have money, it is the money that counts, and money makes money, but what makes money make money?"

And this leads to the question, how does money make money? The answer is simple, it attracts it. Money attracts money. But with the caveat that you have to be smart and guide it to do so.

In order for you to use the Law of Attraction to attract money, you're going to have to learn how money works. Unlike many of the experts out there, I will not say that that money magically attracts money because it doesn't. It attracts money because it enables you to have the means by which to gain more money. Sure, there may be some metaphysical stuff out there on a higher level—isn't there always?—but at the basic level this is how it works. Money equals resources. Resources most of the time—but not always—equal a way for you to earn more money.

Take the stock market for example. If you have the money to buy a stock and you sell it higher than you bought it, you attracted money and you not only attracted it , but you earned it. The same thing goes for farming. If you have the money to buy the seeds, the equipment and what-not, if everything goes well, you will have the means to earn more than your investment. It's just basic business.

Of course, we live in an imperfect world and things do not always work out to our advantage so there is no guarantee of anything. You may not always earn money on your investments; however, having money allows you to get into the game. What you do from then on is up to you. And if you keep a good attitude and know what you want, you will find a way to succeed.

That gets me back to how money works.

While I've briefly discussed how money works on a basic level, I now want to talk it a little more in depth. I want to discuss the meaning of money and how it works on a level other than the obvious. I want to discuss what money can do. Or rather what the *idea* of money can do.

As you probably realize, money is not all there is to wealth. Sure, it's the most basic part, but most people do not strive to become wealthy to simply have money. They want to become wealthy because of what it *means* to be wealthy. It means freedom. It means that a person is perceived differently. It means that doors open and people tip their hats. It means that you are somebody as opposed to all the nobodies without it. It means that you have *arrived* or were already there, so to speak. It means that you have class. It means that people defer to you. It means that you are noticed as someone who is noteworthy. This is the idea of money and as you realize money itself is actually a very small part of it.

When I say that money is a very small part of the idea of money, I mean that you don't really even have to have it. Not really. You just have to *seem* to have it. Or have had it at some point. Take for example European nobility. Many of these people are almost broke, but are still treated with utmost respect simply because of the idea of money. Because of their titles and names, the idea of money is still present even if it isn't in their wallets. Look at con-men who pretend to be wealthy and scam rich widows. They go to all the clubs and parties simply because they pretend to have wealth. And if they are good at the deception, they are accepted. In a similar vein, look at artists and writers. Many of them do not have that much money, but because of what they do, they have a certain something that while not necessarily equal the idea of money, it is very akin to it. It is fame. They are noteworthy and people like to be around noteworthy people.

So it is true that when people say that money attracts money this much is true. But it also attracts opportunities— which many times are more important than money. However, it can also attract many bad things as well. It is like a net that once cast brings all manner of objects back. As with all of the other things I've mentioned some of the bad things come in the form of temptations and bad impulses. This is why one must exercise caution with money. Just as in picking the right stock or planting the right crop. Or committing a crime. The freedom of choice is essential. Just as the author Robertson Davies once wrote, "Where there is a will, there is always two ways."

There are people to whom money is everything. It is all they think about. It controls them. They don't go with the flow. They actively pursue money or go to outlandish means to save it. It means a great deal to them and they would do anything for it. Some of these people are trying to fill a hole in their lives with the money. Others are trying to improve their lives. Regardless, money almost becomes a god to them and without it, they feel they are nothing. Sure, some of them are successful, but without money they are miserable. There are also some people who are misereable even when they have money. This is why it's important to distinguish between actual wealth and having a lot of money.

And on the opposite end of the spectrum, there are those who say that money means nothing to them. In fact, they seem to be repelled by money. However, if the truth be told these people are the same as those people to whom money is everything. They're just the other side of the coin. Their focus is still on money. Many times they are people who have always had easy access to money and take it for granted. Or perhaps, they know all to well how much power and opportunity money can buy and just don't want to be bothered. They would rather have the simple life that they perceive those without money have. However, this is a naïve assumption because if they didn't truly know the power and meaning of money, they wouldn't try so hard to avoid it.

For those of you who are primarily interested in realistically attracting more money, you have to first know how money works and you'll have to figure out what you want out of life and what you want your money to do. All the manifesting and releasing and visualizing won't mean anything if you don't understand the basics. You won't be able to appreciate what you attract unless you truly understand what it can do. You have to also realize that money also has a way of gaining momentum. Once you get in the flow of attracting wealth, more will come. It is like being on a hot streak at a dice table. For some reason, when you're hot, you're hot and once the money starts rolling in, it almost seems to have a mind of its own. But you have to let it. You cannot force it. This is why hard work is not always a way to success. If it is forced and you hate doing what you do, even if your bank account grows large, you will not be happy. Wealth has to do with more than just money.

The biggest thing to realize when thinking about how money works is that no really knows what money truly means. Sure, people know on a superficial level, but due the many layers of it and the individual meanings that people put onto it, no really knows. In fact, I would almost say that it means something different to most people. To some it may mean freedom. To others it may mean a burden. To others, it's everything. To some it's nothing. One thing for certain though is that when you have money, you will be able to easily get more money. It is truly like a magnet due to all the opportunities and resources that it can provide.

WEALTH IS NOT THE SAME THING AS MONEY

While we touched on this subject briefly in the previous chapter, I thought the concept of wealth needed a bit more of an explanation. Wealth is not the same thing as money. Now, of course, everyone will say on the surface that wealth is not everything. They will say that more things are needed in life to be happy than just money. However, the problem is that few people *really* believe this. Saying is one thing, believing is another one entirely.

I'm sure that no will admit to this, but it's true. Regardless of how happy you are, you will always think that you would be happier if you had just a little more money. There's nothing wrong with this. But you have to realize in your heart that wealth alone will not make you happy. Once you do this, money will be much easier to come by. This is because it will be less of a struggle and you will clear a path for it. You have to truly realize and accept that wealth is about a state of well-being and happiness in being yourself. It is about being in tune not only with yourself, but also with the universe.

I already mentioned how money makes money. One of the reasons behind this is not only because money will buy you resources to make more money, but also because once you have some money, money will become less important. You will place less of an emphasis on it. When you do this, it will come easier to make it. This is because you will not be forcing things. You will no longer stress so much about money. You will not be struggling. It will become more fun because you will be able to enjoy your money because you won't be afraid of it or terrified that it will go away. You gain confidence in yourself above all things and this confidence is what will make you even wealthier.

But is this to say that people can be wealthy in things other than money? That they can be wealthy but still be broke financially? Of course. But these people are few and far between. Many people who tell you that they are this way are just trying to make themselves feel better about not having enough money. I'm not saying this is right, but it's true. You have to recognize the truth in order to get past it. Once you do this, you can accept and be grateful for what you have rather than bitter for what you don't.

USE IT OR LOSE IT!

When you set out to attract money, you must do so with the idea that you will use it. While you should not be foolish with it and blow every dime so that you're broke again in no time flat, you should also not put all of it in the bank and let it gather dust while you still live like a pauper. If you choose the latter path, it will be like you didn't even attract it at all. Why even bother? You haven't improved your life one bit. Sure, you might have money in the bank for an emergency, but you'll probably be so desperately afraid of spending it that you'll lose your mind if an emergency actually did arise.

This is why you have to use your money. If you don't, it will become a burden. It will become an obstacle in your life. It will hold you back. It will be something that you have to always work around and protect. It will make your life miserable. If you don't use it, you might as well not even have it.

An example of extreme unneccesary parsimony is illustrated in the story of an old man who lived near me. He was a farmer and even though he owned a large farm, from the looks of him he was always hard up against it. He drove an old truck and lived in an old house which was so run down, he had no indoor plumbing. He was so thrifty wouldn't even allow himself to buy a hamburger at a restaurant. The most he would splurge on was a cup of coffee and that was a rare occasion. He was a real cheap person and his wife was subjected to this kind of behavior throughout their marriage until she died. Of course, eventually he died, too. In a farming accident, as a matter of fact. And surprise, surprise, when the administrators of his estate started going through his accounts, it turned out he wasn't a pauper after. He had over six-hundred thousand dollars in his savings account. Let that sink in. Six-hundred thousand dollars. And this was from a man who wouldn't even buy himself a hamburger or put a toilet in his house. While this may not seem like so much to some people, in reality, it's quite a bit. You have to realize that this was several years back when money was worth more. In addition to this fact, he also didn't have any bills. His farm and farm equipment had also been paid off long before so his actual net worth was actually much greater than the six-hundred thousand dollars. This was just money that was sitting unused in a bank. However, you would never have known it to see him. He had so thoroughly convinced everyone (and himself too, probably) of how broke he was that everyone was surprised at how much money he had. They were also a little shocked that he had been so cheap when he could have afforded himself and his wife a much easier and better life. In fact, his memory became somewhat tainted because before he had died, he had been thought of a poor simple farmer, but after he died, he was viewed as a tightwad.

And guess what happened to the money? His daughter inherited it and spent a lot of it remodeling the house—which is what he should have done considering the money went for it anyway. In his mind, this man thought he was poor. As a result he *was* poor. The amount of money he had had nothing to do with his situation. He could have had six-million in the bank and he would have been just as broke in his mind. This is why you have to appreciate what you have. You have to use the money you are fortunate enough to earn.

With this in mind, it should be fairly obvious that just as you can mentally be a pauper with loads of money, you can also do the opposite and be wealthy in your mind with just a little money. In other words, you can be rich with must less. All you have to do is enjoy your money. It's an insult to what you have been blessed with if you do not use it. Of course, you must use it wisely, but you have to use it. You shouldn't spend it on frivolous things, but you shouldn't hoard it away either. There is a balance to be achieved between parsimony and frivolity. Even though many people never find it, it is possible. You just have to enjoy it.

I used the story of the old farmer to illustrate the fact that money is meant to be used. You should be cautious with it and not spend it foolishly, but you should not cling to it so desperately that you become a miserable old tightwad. If you do, you will become locked up and it will be even more difficult to get. It is money. It can be replaced. It is meant to be enjoyed. It is like a toy that is bought and put away unused because it might be worth something later on. Because, like a toy, it has a purpose and if that purpose is not met, it ceases to be what it is—a means to attain more and be happy.

As I mentioned earlier there's a phrase that says something to the fact that, "Wealth unused might as well not exist." This is my point exactly. If you don't use it, you'll lose it. And if you don't literally lose it, you aren't using it. So isn't that almost the same thing?

IF YOU WANT TO DO IT, YOU CAN

You know the old cliché, if you think you can't do something, you can't? It's so true. But the opposite is also true. If you think you can do something, you can. You just have to find a way.

This is entirely what the Law of Attraction is about. Imagining something that you want and being able to do it. I firmly believe if you truly know what you want and are positive about it, you will see opportunities that you never knew existed. Opportunities and ideas will come to you. A way will be made. Whether or not you act on them is up to you. However, the path is there for you to take.

So many people get caught up thinking that they can't do something. They think that something they want to do is an impossibility. And I'll grant you, sometimes they may think this with good reason due to their personal circumstances, however, they should never give up. They should also reevaluate what it is they want to do. For example, do they want to climb Mt Everest? Or do they simply want to get to the top? Do they want to work their way up in a company to a senior position or do they want to just get a senior position? A lot of what you can accomplish is in how you look at it and the specifics involved. The way that may be presented to you may not be exactly the way you envisioned; however, it is still an end to a means. It's going to give you what you want. However, you may not want to take it. This is okay. Just be aware that opportunities come in many different ways. Sometimes it truly is a case of "be careful what you wish for, because you just might just get it." But not always.

People should try to achieve the achievable before they attempt the unachievable because this will make the seemingly unachievable more attainable. They will be less likely to be discouraged if they experience some easy victories on their way to their ultimate goal. In other words, don't spend your life trying to do the impossible because all the stuff that you could have accomplished will go neglected. Always shoot high, but don't forget to pick the flowers along the way.

You just have to realize that good things can happen for you. You just have to believe and you have to look at them in the right way. You need to think them through and not sell yourself or your abilities short. Sure you may want to be an award winning singer, but don't you want to earn those awards rather than someone simply handing them to you? You can do anything you want. You just have to believe. And you have to have a good attitude.

ATTRACTING WEALTH—YOU HAVE TO BE READY

Everyone wants to be rich.

Or at least most people do. However, what many people don't realize is that with success comes a lot of responsibility. While you'll have many more wonderful opportunities that will become available to you due to your increased resources, you'll also be presented with temptations and problems you never even knew existed or thought you would never have to deal with. When you become rich, while it's true that your money problems can go away, sometimes the other difficulties in your life don't. This is why when you use the Law of Attraction, you have to ready for wealth because when it comes, it may come roaring in so suddenly that you can get overwhelmed.

I know you've heard stories about lottery winners that go broke. In fact it happens so much that it's almost a cliché. You've also heard about people who inherit lots of money only to end up on welfare. About people who have very successful businesses or are successful musicians or athletes or actors but end up going bankrupt because they overspent. This is exactly what I'm talking about. You have to respect your money. You have to prepare yourself for it—mentally and spiritually. It's not all about gold chains and jet skis. Wealth attracts wealth and once it starts rolling in, it will be even easier for more to roll in. However, just as this is the case, waste also begets waste. Squandering attracts squandering as well and if you are sloppy with the money you are so fortunate to be awarded with, it will run out. This is why you have to be ready. You don't want to be the multi-millionnaire who went broke because he couldn't stop buying islands, do you? Just as money attracts more money, once you start turning the cycle around and start going into the hole, poverty can also gain momentum and attract more its kind. Wealth works both ways in that regard.

As I alluded to earlier, you have to be ready for wealth and how you get ready is simple. You make a plan about what you're going to do with your money when it comes. This will not only help you to get ready for the wealth you're going to attract but will also help you manifest and visualize what you want. You can write down this plan if you want. It doesn't have to be anything formal. What you do is start to write down what you want and then write its price. This will help you get a perception of exactly what things cost. Look up the prices online if you have to get an idea of what things cost. This might depress you a little but it shouldn't. It should help you become realistic on what your money can do when you get it. You will know that if you come into a million dollars that you won't be able to buy all your family and friends houses and Rolls Royces without going broke. If you're fully aware of what your money can do, you will also know what it cannot do. This is the difference between people who progressively become more and more successful and those who ride high for a while but end up falling on their faces. If you know what you want out of life, isn't it just as important to know just how much you need in order to attain it? This will only help you to attract it.

This may sound a little contradictory to what some of the experts tell you but in reality, it isn't. If you want to know how the Law of Attraction works in regards to money, you have to understand its power. And to understand its power, you also have to understand its weakness. You cannot go into attracting wealth blindly. You have to ready for its full power because when it starts coming, it will come fast. Money is a tool and getting it is just part of equation. You also have to know how to use it. You can either let it overpower you because you don't understand it and what it's capable of or you can learn to harness its strength. Money can make you and it can also break you if you're not careful. You can overspend with hundreds of millions of dollars in the bank just as easily as you can with a few hundred. When it comes to money, relativity is the key. Going broke or getting rich is just the end result of your attitude towards money.

WHY DO YOU WANT TO BE RICH?

I know this is a pretty obvious question, but I think that before you set out to attain riches, it's a good idea to know why you want to be rich in the first place. There's no right or wrong answer because this is such a personal question, but it's good to know why and what is driving you towards this goal. This way, you'll truly know when you've attained what you're trying to achieve.

Many people who are rich have no real idea why they wanted to be rich. In fact, many of them never even wanted to be rich in the first place. They either inherited the money or just fell into it accidentally and then found themselves in a very comfortable position. Others are constantly struggling and striving to increase their wealth. They work long hours and deprive themselves of pleasure and joy just to attain more money. And then there are some who work to attain money as though it is some sort of score in the big game of life. With higher amounts of money, they see themselves as having a higher score and, in essence, this allows them to see themselves as winners in life. Some people want it for security and some others want it for status. And lastly, there are people who try to use money to fill some sort of void that is lacking in their life. They think everything will be okay if they just have some money. They think that everything in their life will work out if they just have the money issues straightened out.

As I was saying, and I'm not judging, there is no right or wrong answer to this. I personally think that wealth is an incredible tool and you should be careful what values you ascribe to it. In essence, one should never lose track of the idea that it is just money and what you do with it is up to you. In the big scheme of things, it won't make you or break you, but it can definitely help you if use it properly. You should look at it as something that you always deserve and not place so much emphasis on having it—or on not having it. If you do this, it will come much more easily because you won't be trying so hard.

So the bottom line is to know why you want to be rich so you'll know when you've attained your goal. You shouldn't have to work so hard at it either. Just let it come and know what you want it to do for you. This is part of knowing what you want. If you don't know what you want, you'll never know when you get it.

IF YOU DON'T KNOW WHERE YOU'RE GOING, YOU'LL END UP SOMEWHERE ELSE

Since we've talked about what you want out of life, we also need to talk about where you want to go in life. Whether it's in your career or in your life in general, it's crucial to have a sense of direction. This is because if you don't know where you're going, you'll probably end up somewhere you don't want to be. This not only applies to your work but also your homelife as well.

You have to know where you want to go in life if you truly want to be happy. Sure, sometimes you'll luck into a good situation, but most of the time, you'll just end up in a place that is merely acceptable. This is not only true when you're traveling, but also in your life as well. Most likely, if you start out with a vague idea of what it is that you want to do, you'll probably follow the path of least resistance into a job that will pay just enough to make it worth the hassle to stay in it. You've heard of the Peter Principle? It's an idea put forth by Dr. Lawrence J. Peter and Raymond Hill that says that, "In a hierarchy every employee tends to rise to his level of incompetence." In a nutshell, it says that people advance to a level to where they are unable to do their job. And this is where they stay because they can no longer make any progress. Well, what I'm talking about with always taking the path of least resistance in your life is is like the Peter Principle in reverse. You settle into you comfort zone where you are quite competent and you can go on autopilot. You don't necessarily like where you've ended up, but you justify it by the fact that you're getting paid reasonably well and it's easy and comfortable. You'll ignore the long term effect it has on both you and your family and you'll slowly lose any idea of what it is that you'll want to do. The same thing applies to marriage or relationships or your house or car. You'll just end up somewhere or with someone who is just good enough. And sometimes barely.

Of course, this is a worst case scenario, but it happens every day to many people. And this also applies to the place you work as well. Maybe you like your job, but you hate the company. You'll rationalize it in the same fashion just to justify your continuing to work there. After all, the devil you know is better than the one you don't. Especially if he pays well.

If you want to be happy in your work life and your home life, you'll not only have to do something you like but you'll also have to work somewhere you like. Whether this means working for yourself or taking a plunge into the unknown, you'll have to make a move if you don't want to spend your career in an unhappy place. It might even mean that you may have to start putting yourself out there and taking a chance on love as well as life. Life is too short to spend it unhappy. And there's nothing more unhappy than a person who hates his job and the place he works. Or his home life. You may try to compartmentalize but you'll only be able to do this for so long before the walls begin to break down.

I'm sure that I'm not telling you anything you don't already know. If you dislike your job or homelife, no one knows this better than you. What I'm telling you is that there is a way out. No matter how much you have been brainwashed into thinking that this is the end of the road, there are other possibilities. Not just in where you are in your career but in your personal life as well. You weren't born in this place, were you? So why should you die (both figuratively and literally) there?

YOU HAVE TO HAVE STANDARDS

Whenever I talk about the Law of Attraction, I inevitably talk about how you need to know what you want in order to get it. This is very important. I've also talked about how you need to know where your life is going and how you have to make conscious efforts in this regard. Regardless, both ideas boil down to knowing exactly what you want out of life. However, what is just as important is to also know what you *don't* want out of life. Just as you have to be self-aware enough to know your needs and wants, you also have to aware enough to know what you absolutely do not want to do.

It should be obvious why I'm telling you this, but I'll elaborate anyway. The reason why you have to know what you don't want out of life is because if you don't recognize what this, you may inevitably end up doing it. You won't know what you don't like and you'll just drift into it. This is a very similar concept to the one that I mentioned in the previous chapter. However, in that chapter, I'm talking about the path of least resistance and how you'll many times end up situations that are just blah. In this one, I'm talking about how, if you're not careful, you'll end up doing a job or dating someone that you absolutely can't stand. And you know from the beginning that this particular state of affairs is not a good one for you. It's just somehow or another, you allow yourself to fall into it. Maybe it's because you feel you have something to prove to yourself? Maybe it's because you look at it as a challenge? Regardless, doing things that you know you don't like will only make you miserable. This is where the idea of standards comes into play.

It's like this. Has the idea of doing a particular kind of job filled you with such dread that you couldn't sleep at night?

Of course, it has. But then came a certain point in your life when you were broke and absolutely needed to work. Suddenly the specter of this job that you hated started to loom larger and larger in your psyche. You could always do that for a little bit, you thought, even though you knew you would hate it. You would put it out of your mind, but then after a while, all other possiblities become smaller and eventually this one dreaded job seems like it's your only choice. It's then that you cave and do it. This has certainly happened to me on more than one occasion and I know that I'm no exception.

But in my case, knowing what I didn't want to do was secondary to not allowing myself to do it. When it came to jobs, my standards were low. I was desperate at times and would do anything for money. I was taken advantage of by many employers simply because I allowed them to do so. I always thought that if I started low and worked hard, I would get promoted because they would see just what I was capable of. I was right except for the promotion part. They saw what I was capable of and how I was willing to work for less. This is why people who were less qualified than me would inevitably get promoted over me. It's because the employers knew that these people would quit rather than work for nothing.

But what does this have to do with the Law of Attraction? Everything. If you're miserable in a job or life situation then more misery will be attracted to your life. The only way you can break this cycle is to be aware. I know that many people are not aware that they hate a particular situation or job until they're in it. This is why you need to know your needs beforehand and when you see that something is not right for you; you need to get out of it as quickly as possible. Life is too short to be spent being miserable.

This is where standards come in. You have to have standards. If you're unwilling to do something, don't hesitate to say no. Does the idea of manual labor bother you? Don't do it. Or if you don't have a choice, do it for as short a time as possible while concentrating on attaining the job that you really want. Do you become repulsed at the idea of dating a male chauvinist pig? Don't date him. Even if he is a multi-gazillionaire. Never settle for less. Always look for something better that will make you happy. Sure, sometimes your standards might be out of line with realistic thinking and have to be adjusted, but it's still important to have them.

You must have standards because life is about choices. If your standards are too low, then you will make the wrong choices and become a miserable person. It's never too late to change. You can always do better. Never forget that.

KNOW A GOOD THING WHEN YOU SEE IT

Even if you don't know what you want to do in life, there's comes a time when you'll ultimately do something, usually accidentally, that you like. You'll find a job or activity that you love. It will be the perfect fit. It might not pay the most money in the world or it may not have that much status, but it will suit you and you'll be happy. It might even be a person that you date. On paper, they may not look like much, but in your heart, you know that this person is the right one for you. However, if it's a job, if you're like me, you'll probably eventually quit it because you're not making enough money or have enough benefits. Or it will be something like a relationship or opportunity that you stumble into and like so much that it scares you. It just can't be true so you run from it. This is a big mistake. This is how you know what you really want. This is your gut instinct telling you when you're knocking on the right door and that you've arrived at the right place. You should never ignore it. Many people are so oblivious that they never recognize when good things happen. However what's worse is when they recognize it and then turn it away.

Money, benefits or prestige, while good in and of themselves, are not enough to sustain a happy career or a happy life. You have to enjoy what you're doing and enjoy where you're doing it. You have to enjoy the person you're dating. You have to feel good about yourself and this comes from without almost as much as it does from within. If you like what you're doing and where you're doing it, figure out a way to use it to make more money or gain prestige. The same thing goes with relationships. Figure out a way to make the relationship work. Don't approach it from the other way around. Don't take a job that you know you're probably going to dislike and try to make it into something else. The money and prestige will not sustain you. It might help sustain your lifestyle, but the misery will bleed over. A job or place that you dislike can only be short term things in your career. The same thing goes for relationships and friendships and business opportunities as well. Don't just do something because it just seems like the right thing to do. Do it because it feels right and it makes you happy. This is how the Law of Attraction will begin to show dividends. If you're unhappy, you'll just attract more unhappiness. Remember happiness and wealth gain momentum, but so does unhappiness and poverty.

I know that when it comes to your career, sometimes you will have to suffer through things you don't like just to pay the bills. Most people have to do this. However, you should always keep your eye out for something better. Also, don't date a wealthy zero just because you think it makes you look like a big shot. Being around people and jobs that are bad for you isn't going to help you. If you stick around any longer than you have to, their effects can be devastating.

THE GREAT TRUTH

If you're going to allow the Law of Attraction to help you, you're going to have to both recognize and accept the great truths of life. The reason why you have to recognize and accept them is because you need to understand the things that you can't do anything about. This will enable you to move beyond them so you can live your life and concentrate on the things that you can do something about. In other words, if you can understand the things that you can't do anything about, then you will stop worrying about them and wasting your time with them.

And what are these great truths? In reality, there is only one. There is only one thing that you cannot get around. That you cannot ultimately do anything about. The great truth is that at some point everyone has to die. No matter what you do, when it's your time, it's your time.

And that's pretty much it.

Other than that most other things are optional. Even taxes. Sure there are consequences to some of the other situations out there, but you have control over your actions. And you have some control over the outcome. Death is something you will not win against so why waste the time and effort worrying about it? Once you do this, you will free yourself up to all the other possibilities in the world. It's just a matter of you picking what you want and when you want it. Do you want a Mercedes? You can have it. Sure, you may say that you can't afford it, but you have to understand that there is always a way. This is where the Law of Attraction comes in. If you truly want something, and you know what you want, you will figure out a way to make it happen. It's that simple. Have you ever tried to remember something and couldn't quite bring it up to the front of your mind? No matter how hard you tried, it just wouldn't come to the surface? How about a lost object? Have you ever looked everywhere and had no luck? No matter how hard you try to force yourself to find it, it just becomes more and more lost to you. But what happens once you give up and take a break? It miraculously occurs to you. The thought comes back and the object shows up. This is a perfect analogy of the principles of the Law of Attraction. You have to release your desires and let the universe or God, if you will, take care of them.

I know there are some people out there will say that this is a downer of an idea. And really, death is a downer; however, I choose to see the upside. If you knew there was only one thing out there in life that you could not change, wouldn't it be a relief to you? That out of all the possiblities that life has to offer, there is only one that you do not have control over? You can do practically anything you want in life. You just have to realize that the only thing holding you back is you and your outlook on life.

One of the biggest problems that people who are frustrated in their attempts to attain the seemingly unattainable is that due to their failed efforts they begin to think that their goals are unachievable. This is untrue; they would be achievable if they only knew how to achieve them. It is not the goal that is evading them; it is the way to attain the goal.

So the moral of this story is that anything is possible except the one great truth. Once you can understand this, you are on your way. You can do anything you want because you control your destiny. It's not your goals that are evading you; it's the way to achieve them. If you can just lighten up and let things come to you, you will pull through. There is only one thing that you can't do anything about, so how about you start concentrating on all the countless other things you do have some level of control over?

THE CYCLE OF DEBT

Money can be a tremendous tool in attaining and attracting more riches, but it can also be a horrible weight that can bring you down. No, I'm not talking about the terrors of the responsibility of having large sums of money, I'm talking about spending money that you don't have. I'm talking about the idea of agreeing to spend money you plan on earning in the future with the promise of paying it back for something you're going to use now. I'm talking about debt and it has a cycle. The problem is that if you're not careful, this cycle will permanently ruin you.

If you want to really understand money I think it's very important that also understand debt. You need to think about what it is. It is using money that you haven't earned yet. It's about spending money that you don't have. It is about borrowing something that does not belong to you and slowly giving it back with interest. When it comes to buying a house or a car, it is about agreeing that you will give over a certain percentage of what you earn back to the lender for a certain period of time until what you borrowed (and the interest) is paid back. It is about selling a portion of your life. It is about selling your freedom because over that period of time, you're saying that you will do what it takes to make that payment. Regardless of whether or not you really want to do what it's going to take to do it.

Now, I know that some debt can't be avoided especially on big ticket items like cars and houses; however, what can be done is to go into this debt differently. You need to go into it with the idea that you're going to pay it off as quickly as possible. It is about you buying your freedom back as soon as you can. It is not about paying the minimum and hoping for the best. It is about taking control of your life and your finances so that you'll owe no one anything and you'll be free to live your life as you wish. At least within reason.

I know that this is commonsense stuff but so few people really get it. They are fooled by money managers and other experts into thinking that they can finance their lives. They say that you can pay the minimum and get by but this isn't true. All you're doing when you listen to this sort of advice is burying yourself further. Remember that many of these experts make money when you go into debt. It is in their best interests for you to borrow money. Always look at the source of financial advice and determine if the person asking you to do something that is to your detriment has something to gain before you commit yourself to anything.

Before you can become debt-free, you first need to understand the cycle of debt. You know the cycle I'm talking about, right? I'm talking about the one where you start off with no cash and then you borrow to have something, maybe pay it off and then borrow more money to buy something else because what you just bought has worn out. In this cycle you never ever own anything of value and you're always in debt. You may get a few months or few years of freedom if you're lucky when your car lasts past your last payment or you live long enough to get your house paid off. However, this is rarely the case.

The point is, if you can ever get the place where you can get your purchases paid off and they last long enough for you to save money, you will begin to turn the cycle around. If you can become debt-free, you can get into a cycle where you save your money, buy what you need for cash and then when it wears out, use cash again to buy what you need once more. You're in control and you're not beholding to anyone.

If you can just look at the way people in the good old days used to view finances, you'll get an idea of what I'm talking about. You can also look at people from underprivileged countries who immigrate to wealthier nations for examples. In the old days, people would save money to buy things. They would borrow only if necessary. The reason why this was because it was much harder to get a loan. People were farmers and self-employed artisans so their income was unstable. They wanted to avoid debtor's prison if at all possible so they would make sacrifices and do without in order to buy what they needed. The same thing goes with immigrants from poor countries. Have you ever noticed how many of them always pay with cash and are essentially debt-free even though they have been in this country for a very short time? This is because they can't take out loans because they have no credit history, but also because it's not in their way of doing things. In their countries, it is much harder to get a loan so they wait and pay cash. This way they start out the cycle in the right way. They start out paying cash. This is why many of them seem to be wealthier than the native citizens. And to be honest, they *are* wealthier because they have a financial freedom that most of the native citizens haven't enjoyed since their teenage years.

The thing you need to understand is that debt is bad. Sure is it is sometimes necessary and sometimes it is manageable, but longlasting debt is bad. Always. You should always work to pay everything off as soon as possible. Remember that debt attracts more debt. The same thing is true with paying cash. If you can start paying cash for things, you'll be amazed at how much more you'll be able to buy with cash. This is when you're truly in control of your money and when you'll really begin attracting wealth.

BASIC FINANCIAL POWER

Just as the cycle of debt is a very important thing to understand when you're wondering about how money works and how crucial a part of the Law of Attraction plays in it, you also need to understand another fundamental concept. The thing about this concept is that it is true whether you believe in the Law of Attraction or not. The gist of the concept is basically if you want real financial power, don't overextend yourself and pay your bills on time.

It's true. If you live in the low end of your means and pay your bills on time, you will always be on firm financial footing. And as we've talked about earlier regarding the Law of Attraction, when you're on firm financial footing, you will attract many more opportunities to increase you wealth. While it seems like such a simple and commonsense concept, you would be amazed at how many people ignore it.

It's very simple. If you don't overextend yourself with debt, you will have plenty of money for those emergencies that can otherwise derail you financially. If you pay your bills on time and don't borrow too much at any one given time, you will have good credit so that you can borrow money when you really need it. Hopefully, you will get to the place where you won't have to borrow money, but in the meanwhile it's good to have options.

What is your current income? How much do your current bills total? If you're struggling, you'll find that you've both overextended yourself and you're having a hard time staying current on your bills. Why is this? Sometimes events happen in life that cause us to go more in debt than we need to. However, many times, it's just the allure of material things that do us in. If you want the Law of

Attraction to work for you, as counter-intuitive as this may sound, you have to almost become indifferent to money and material things. You have to be able to take it or leave it while still manifesting your desires. The reason why this is that if you cannot turn off your material desires or at least hold them at bay, you will never get into a position of financial power. You're always going to overextend yourself and you're always going to have trouble paying your bills. In other words, don't bite off more than you chew. Regardless of what anybody tells you. Remember what I said in an earlier chapter about looking for the motivations behind the people giving you financial advice? If someone is telling you that you can afford something that you know you can't, chances are they are benefitting in some way from the sale.

But what if you're already in a position of debt? What can you do to turn it around? I will lay out a simple plan in the next chapter, but I'll state it briefly here. Assess your outgoing money and stop spending on anything that you don't need. Just cut unnecessary spenditures out cold-turkey. If you eat out a lot, cut it out. If you spend lots of money on coffee, make your own. It's cheap. Whatever you do, you can do it more inexpensively. Unless you're already at the bottom, you can always figure out ways to save money. And if you're at rock bottom, do everything as cheaply as possibly until you turn your finances around. Once you pay off some of this debt and turn around the cycle of debt, you can once again indulge yourself but in a more restrained manner I hope. But in the short term, you'll have to pull back on the spending and start paying off your debt. Remember you've been having your good times. Now it's time to get caught up on your bills. Once you start paying them off and as long as you don't take on more, they will soon fall like dominos. You just have to keep in mind that the idea of credit is merely that you're promising someone that you'll pay them back in the future for something they're giving you today. If you keep promising people you'll pay them back, you'll not only never have money of your own because you're essentially selling your life to them, but you're just also flat out making too many promises. Promises that you'll eventually be unable to keep.

So if you want power, just keep the basics in mind. Don't spend what you don't have and make sure that you pay what you owe. If you can master this simple little idea, the majority of your money woes will disappear faster than your cash does now.

A SIMPLE PLAN TO GET OUT OF DEBT

Most people will at some time get themselves into debt. This is a fact. Whether or not they stay in debt is completely up to them.

As I mentioned earlier, there is a cycle of debt. It can either be against you or for you. Sure, there are some unforeseen circumstances that happen in life, but if you can get a good foothold on your finances, you've won most of the battle.

In order to turn around the cycle of debt, you first have to get out of debt, or at the least, reduce it significantly. There is no magic to this. You have to stop spending your money on purchases that aren't necessary and start paying off your debt. Whatever it takes to accomplish this, you have to do it.

It is very simple to get into debt and very simple to get out of it. While I'm no economist, it all breaks down to basic math. Don't spend more than you make, save as much as you comfortably can and pay off your debts as quickly as possible. After you're on firm financial footing, then you can start wisely enjoying your money and building wealth.

When figuring out what you need to do get out of debt, the first thing you'll need to do is break down just exactly where your money is going. Make a list of all your expenses. A spending diary, if you will. Most people who are continuously in debt usually don't have a clue as to where most of their money goes. They just pay it out. If you can start recognizing where it's actually going, you can stop the leaks. Do you eat out a lot? Start eating more cheaply at home. Some people will say that it's cheaper to eat out, but this largely depends on what you eat and the number of people in your family. You can always improve regardless of your situation. If you're in dire financial shape, you just didn't arrive there because you were careful with your money. Obviously. Tighten your belt and start turning things around. Make a game of it. Look for opportunities to save money. Figure out where you're getting ripped off. Or at least where you feel you are and do something about it.

After you figure out where your money is going, you can start directing it into paying off your debts. Always pay your debts first before your money disappears. This may be tough at first, but this is one of the foundations to getting out of debt. Start off paying individual bills down. Start with the small ones, the easy ones. Pay everything you can on them and then work your way up to bigger ones. The next thing you know you're paying extra on your house. And after that, you'll find yourself paying your house off. It is simple math. The more you pay the less you owe. And the less you owe, the more you'll be able to save. When you start turning things around—and it will be painful at first—your life will improve. Especially when you start making headway on your bills.

I know that this will be very difficult for most people to do, but once you do it and get out of debt, you'll find that you will begin to think twice about buying things you don't need. You will save money and the relief you feel over having plenty of money left at the end of the month will be amazing to you. You'll feel like a kid again. Once you do this, you will be happier and you will find that instead of attracting more debt, you are attracting more money. Worries will be lifted from your mind. Money in your pocket and savings account will do wonders for your health as well as mental well-being. Worrying about money is one of the worst things that you can do and if you can do anything to reduce that worry, you'll be that much better off.

Remember the more money you have, the more money you'll attract. Get rid of the debt and everything else will fall into place.

ARE YOU IN A PATTERN?

Look at your life and evaluate it. Are you miserable? Are you in debt? Do you feel bad about yourself? Or do you feel great and think that everything's coming up roses? Regardless, if you're in either situation, you're in a pattern. It goes without saying that it's better to be in the latter pattern than it does the former.

The Law of Attraction works anyway that you allow it. If you are in a pattern of debt, you will attract more debt. If you're in a pattern of misery, than you will attract more misery. Whatever you're feeling in your life is what you will attract. This is why it's so important to be positive. Your feelings and actions have momentum. Good or bad will bring more of its kind. This is why if bad things are happening to you, you have to laugh through the tears until you can turn the pattern around. You have to look on the bright side until there is nothing but bright side to look at. The world around you is mainly a matter of perspective and if you can just change your perspective for the positive, your perspective will not only change, but your world will change too.

Think of this way: Are you a wasteful person? If you are, you're going to attract more waste. It will become a habit and it will just continue to grow. Are you a stingy person? You'll just get stingier. However, if you're generous, you'll see that you'll attract generosity. It's that simple. Life is a pattern. You just have to decide what pattern you want. It really is that simple. It keeps successful people successful and poor people poor. It's true.

So what pattern are you in? Is it a good one? Or is it a bad one?

Once you figure this out, you can make the necessary changes it will take to either change it for the better if it's a bad one or to continue it going along wonderfully if it's a good one.

YOU'RE NOT DOING IT ALL WRONG

Before I tell you anything else, let me assure you that you're okay. You're doing most things right and if you just become more positive, things will work out for you.

But why am I telling you this?

It's like this: Have you ever gotten the feeling that no matter what you do, you're not doing things right? Like when it comes to eating, what you're eating is the wrong thing. Or if you're drinking, you're drinking the wrong thing. Or that you're exercising too little or too much. No matter what it is you're doing, you're just not doing it right. I think this scenario applies to most people.

The problem with most self-help and Law of Attraction books is that they always tell you that you're doing everything wrong in your life without actually telling you how or what exactly you're doing wrong or how you can fix it. You're either doing too much, not enough, or just standing still. There are no standards to judge yourself by. If you're too poor, you're not working hard enough. If you're too rich, you're a selfish person or were born with a silver spoon. With this in mind, just how do you know if you're doing anything right?

The thing is that this same thing happens to other people all the time in their lives as well. Here's an example of this in the real world. I used to be in middle management in a large food manufacturing facility. For some reason the job was overrun by politics and manipulation from other departments which was absolutely ridiculous considering the banal nature of the job. However, I just took it in stride and was sort of bemused by it. Even so, as a result of all this conniving and such, periodically one of the managers would come bursting into my office redfaced and waving his hands in the air (well not actually waving his hands in the air, but this is good for dramatic effect) and exclaim "You're doing your job wrong!"

Of course, I sort of laughed this off at first because it was just so ludicrous. However, over time, I began to notice that some of the other managers were taking notice of this and I began to think that I truly wasn't doing my job right. Even though there was no evidence to suggest that I wasn't. I hit every target and was thought by most people who were directly involved in the results of my job (downstream and upstream, so to speak) to be very competent in my position. Regardless, the hysteria of my manager began to bother me and I started to wrack my brain trying to figure out what I was doing wrong. I couldn't figure it out. It made me self-conscious of everything I did. I began to second-guess myself. I began to wonder if I was just under some sort of illusion that things really were okay. Surely, I wasn't that oblivious. I asked around in the plant to see if I was in the right. People said that things were great. Everything was running smoothly, orders were getting out on time. But still, this manager would continue to periodically come in and say, "You're doing your job wrong!"

Eventually, I had enough and just asked him. "Just how am I doing my job wrong?"

He stopped in his tracks. With a blank look, he said, "I don't know!" and abruptly walked out.

I knew it! I wasn't really doing anything wrong. He was just being manipulated by someone who wanted him to think I was doing everything wrong.

I know this is a riduculous example, but it illustrates perfectly what is wrong with so many self-help books. They convince you you're doing everything wrong and get you hyped up to do it right, then they leave without telling you what you're doing wrong or how exactly to fix it. And most likely, you aren't really doing anything wrong to begin with. As a result of this doubt, it messes up your thinking. Instead of telling you that you are doing everything wrong, you just need a little reassurance that you are okay.

So that's why I'm not going to tell you that you're doing everything wrong, but rather that you're doing most things right. The only guideline you need to establish if you're successful is to know whether you're truly happy and that you're attracting the things you want. Other than that, you shouldn't worry so much that you're doing things wrong. According to the Law of Attraction you attract what you believe and if you believe you're always doing things wrong, it will be that much harder to attract what is right.

MANIFESTING—A PRACTICAL APPROACH

When it comes to the mechanics of utilizing the Law of Attraction, there is nothing more important than manifesting. This is because it is the first big step towards making it happen. If you don't manifest, most likely you're not going to get what you want from the Law of Attraction.

I'm sure that some people are not quite sure of what manifesting is so I'll make a brief explanation. *Manifesting is the act of bringing your wants and desires to life*. It is like writing a grocery list. You decide what you want and then you put it out for the universe to bring back. How you manifest can take on many forms. Some people take a metaphysical approach to manifesting. While I think this isn't wrong, I think that many people have a hard time wrapping their minds around it so that's why I've come up with a more practical way of looking at it. *Manifesting is simply knowing what you want*. Exactly what you want. Then, once you know what you know what you want, you have to know that you can achieve it. Once known, it will become tangible. This is manifesting. When you do this, you will become aware of many opportunities that you didn't know existed. You will see how to accomplish the things that you want out of life. A way to achieve them will be made apparent. This is how the Law of Attraction works. *Once you know, then you can go*.

As I briefly mentioned earlier in the book, a good way to start manifesting is by writing a list of what you want. It's that simple. You make a list of what you want and then you concentrate. The reason why you do this is very obvious. Once you write it down, it becomes real. You are admitting to yourself what you want and deserve. As I told you before, just write down everything you desire. Do you want a better car? Write it down. Do you want a happier family? Write it down. Do you want a better job? Write it down. You look at this list everyday. You revise it if you want. Add to it whenever you like

Now, when I say that you need to write it down, it's not absolutely necessary for you to physically write your wants and desires down. Some people can keep this list in their heads, but writing it down will definitely be easier for most people. Most of us work from lists in many aspects of their lives. Why should this be any different?

When it comes to manifesting, there is still another way of looking at it. Some people look at it as prayer. In a prayer, you ask God for what you want. It may not be material things that you're requesting, but by saying the prayer, you are putting your thoughts into form. You are making them tangible. This is also manifesting.

Almost everyone who is successful manifests in some way or another. Whether they make a plan to achieve a certain goal or they decide that they are going to do something, they are manifesting. They are turning their desire into a tangible object. Whether it is a list or a plan, it is an intention. It is the idea made manifest. It is a very simple thing to understand once you do this. Look at the Empire State Building. Someone had to want to build it, didn't they? This was manifesting. They made a plan and then everything fell into place. Nothing gets started without some form of action by someone.

But how does it work, you ask? Well, as I mentioned before, once you can put your desires into a tangible form and understand what you really want, you can release them (more on releasing later) and let it work in the background. You can wait on the universe or God or whatever religion you believe in to bring it back. Once you know what you want, opportunities will suddenly present themselves. You will see things that you never saw before that will help you achieve your goals. It's simple but very powerful and it works.

Manifesting is a huge part of the Law of Attraction. It's a big first step. It's like moving from idea to action. It's admitting to yourself and the world that you really want and deserve something. It's making what you want real to yourself and once the idea becomes real, it becomes doable and once it becomes doable, it can happen. You have to have faith to manifest, but once you start and are successful, you'll find that it will become much easier.

VISUALIZATION

When you're first starting out manifesting, one of the best things you can do is to learn is the technique of visualization. This will not only help you more closely define what you want, but will also open your imagination up to the possibility of it really happening. It will also help you to see that the sky is the limit and if you can visualize it, you can do it.

Visualizing is a very simple process and you've probably done it since you were a kid. It's very similar to daydreaming except you are an active participant. You are the one who is participating in the action rather than just watching. Athletes do this all the time. You just simply find a quiet place and think about what you want. You imagine yourself doing it. You visualize yourself doing it. You think about the smells, the sights and the feelings of doing it. You imagine the experience. You feel the happy feelings you get from it. This will not only help you recognize the opportunities that are out there that will help you achieve your goals, it will also help you learn to understand and enjoy them before hand. Good feelings attract good feelings.

The great thing about doing this is that it will become much easier as you do it more and more. Pretty soon, you'll be visualizing all sorts of great things for yourself and if you can visualize it, it can happen.

Many people may have trouble at first visualizing what they want because, all too often, as we grow up, we are always encouraged to be realistic and to squelch any dreams and aspirations we have. We are told to settle for less because that's all we can expect. Shoot low and you won't be disappointed, people will tell you. I say to forget all that. If you need help to imagine the things you want, look at catalogs. Look at TV programs that feature the objects of your desires. Anything you can do to bring the objects of your dreams closer to your mind, do it. Don't be afraid to window shop. Don't be afraid to imagine what can actually happen if you have a good attitude and aren't afraid to admit what you want. Looking at things or people you aspire to should never get you down or make you feel less than. You should never feel like you're not good enough when you see things that you want but rather see them as an idea of the possibilities of life. If you have trouble with this, just look around you. Don't people who always go around downtrodden and envious look very small and petty? Do you ever see any successful people who act like this? Very rarely should be your answer. This is your cue. Just because you don't have something now just means that you don't have it yet.

I know that many experts go into elaborate explanations of visualization, but I won't insult your intelligence. Visualization is simply using your imagination to create a mental model of your dreams and desires. It is like a test run. It may not be exactly the same as the real event when it happens, but it will provide a very positive experience. This will make you feel better about yourself and open your mind to all the many great possibilities that the Law of Attraction has to offer.

MYTHS THAT HAVE HELD YOU BACK

If you're like me, as you get older you begin to realize that much of the stuff that has been drummed into you in life is at least partially false.

I know, I know. There's the story about Mark Twain who said that his father seemed like the dumbest man on earth when he was a teenager, but later on, when Twain was older, he noticed how his father had really smartened up.

I think that in reality many times this is the exception to the rule.

However, if you come from a lower income family like mine, you will definitely find that much of the stuff you're taught regarding money and getting ahead is wrong. I refer to these ideas as myths and the sooner you wake up and get over them the better off you'll be.

In my case, the biggest myth I was taught was that hard work will always save you. It will get you ahead. When I was young, I believed this fully. I would work harder than anyone around me because I truly thought that this would really advance me. Needless to say, it didn't. All it got me was more hard work. This is because I *would* work hard. And I would do it without thinking twice. Even if the job was utterly terrible. I would go all out regardless of the task. I would always do my best while the people around me would either give a lackluster effort or sit around and watch me kill myself. If you think about it, if you had an employee like me, why would you want them to leave a job that no one else wants to do? Why would you promote me? Without me, who would do the hard work?

It was around this time that I began to notice that the people who did get promoted were the ones who were smart enough to stand back and let me do all the hard work while they took the credit. In this case, hard work definitely didn't get me ahead. It kept me behind. Unless you're working for yourself, hard work is usually its own reward.

Another myth that held me back was that I was always taught that life was a struggle to survive. You have to scratch it out just to exist. And this is what I did early on. I scratched it out. I had low expectations for myself and they were usually met. I never thought that I would ever be able to earn lots of money and I was right. I wasn't ever able to. That is until I got over this myth. Once I did, I began to realize that the sky was the limit. The only thing that had held me back was myself.

I think you get my point here. I'm not going to keep going into the different myths because each person's life experience is unique. However, we all can look back to things that have been told to us by our families and teachers that have lowered our expectations out of life. If you can't, just take a moment and think about it. Think about why you think you can't do something. Who told you that you can't? Think about why something that you want to do is impossible. Where did you get that idea? You'll soon realize that you just didn't think of this stuff on your own. What you need to do is when you think of why something is impossible, evaluate why this is. Then come up with a plan to make it possible. It happens for some people, right? Why can't it happen for you? It might not happen in the same way, but if it is possible, it is possible for you.

If you really want to do something, you can do it. However, if you really don't want to do something you will find any excuse you can to not do it. Perhaps this is the case when you think you can't do something. If it is, just admit that you can't do it and stop trying to find excuses. If you do this too much, you'll find excuses why you can't do anything. You'll attract the inability to do anything. Know what you want and what you don't want and be able to differentiate. This is very important.

Everyone has ideas they have been taught that holds them back. Each person's experience is different. The myths that hold you back may be completely different from the myths that held me back. Nevertheless, they are equally as destructive. I know that the people who have taught us this stuff have not done it out of malice. They have taught it because it's the only thing they know. Like us, they were victims of bad information. But unlike them, we know better.

Myths can only ruin your life if you keep letting them ruin it. When you think you can't do something ask yourself why not. I'm pretty sure that it's just because either you don't really want to do something or because someone has told you that you can't. Your job is to tell yourself that regardless of what your source of information is, there is nothing holding you back from achieving whatever it is that you want to achieve.

YOU HAVE TO BE THANKFUL—REGARDLESS

Have you ever been told over and over again how wonderful some food is or how great some amusement park is and then you go only to find yourself disappointed? Or have you ever read so-so and horrible reviews of a book or movie, but went ahead and read or watched it anyway only to be surprised at how good it was? You're not alone.

With that in mind, think about this: Have you ever given someone a present that you spent a lot of time and care on just to have it rejected as not being good enough? Of course, you have. This has happened to all of us. However, when this happens, do you ever want to give this person anything else? I didn't think so. You're also probably a little resentful toward them, too if you're honest with yourself.

This is why you should adopt a basic rule of always being thankful for what you get out of life. If you are not thankful for what God, the universe or whatever/whoever has given you, why should you be given anything else? You don't know everything and you don't know the greater plan surrounding it. In fact, you never know how things will turn out and you should never be so shortsighted to write something off because you never know if it could turn into something really great. Sure, what you receive might not be exactly what you want, but it could possibly turn into more than you ever dreamed. Remember, you're not really in control of the universe so you shouldn't be so arrogant as to think that you're too good for what you have been given.

This is a basic tenet of utilizing the Law of Attraction. You must be thankful. For everything. Even the small things. Even the mundane things. Everything matters and everything is worthy of thanks. If you can't think of anything to be thankful for, be thankful for being able to get out of bed in the morning. Be thankful for being alive. After you start doing this, you will begin to see all the little things in your life that are right and good. You will also stop taking so much for granted.

Your opinions of most things in life are a matter of perspective. Without trying to sound like a relativist, your idea of good and bad mainly depends on your own personal experience. If you're always used to extremely wonderful things happening to you in life, when something mediocre happens to you, you will probably take it for granted. On the other hand, if you're always used to bad things happening, you will probably think something that's not really that great is outstanding. This is why you have to be thankful for everything regardless of your perspective. It will not only improve your attitude because you will begin to truly see just how wonderful the things you receive are, but you will also show that you're capable of recognizing the good things that you're granted and that you're worthy of receiving more.

As is the case with many people, at first you may have to step outside of yourself to do this. It may be tough for some people to make the realization that nothing in this life is guaranteed. Life itself is a gift. If you can start being thankful, then you will start sending out a vibe of appreciation. Don't you want to give more to people who appreciate it than you do to people who take your gifts for granted?

This is how the Law of Attraction works. Be thankful and the universe will give you more. It's that simple.

YOUR LIFE IS YOUR OWN

Have you ever gone through life thinking about how you would like to do something but you won't take that first step because you're afraid of what other people might think? While this is probably a good thing if you want to strip off all your clothes and run through a police station, this kind of thinking can be very damaging when it comes to other areas of your life. If you're not careful, you'll live your life entirely according to other people's expectations of you. Or more importantly, you'll live your life according to what you *think* are other people's expectations of you. When you do this, you'll never know what you really want out of life and you'll never be truly happy. This is where the concept of *releasing* comes in. This is when you stop worrying so much and stop trying to control everything. This is when you become who you really are.

We'll get a little more in depth when it comes to the concept of releasing in the next chapter. However, there are many different ways to look it. Some people say it is just letting go of your worries and going with the flow. Some people say that is just accepting that you are not in control of the world. Some people say it is just loosening up. Others even say that releasing is the same as "leaving it in God's house" or "que sera sera." Regardless how you look at it, it is about not worrying and letting nature take its course. It is about acceptance that whatever happens is what is supposed to happen. It's about not fooling yourself into thinking that you can really control anything. Sure, you can try and maybe you'll be successful some of the time, but really, in the long run, you can only do so much. Things always take their own course eventually.

We all do things in life that we don't necessarily want to do because we know people are counting on us to do them. This is an accepted part of life. Maybe you didn't really want to go to college, but you did so because your parents insisted. Maybe you didn't want to go to visit your grandmother, but your parents insisted. However, these sorts of situations usually work out for the best because they are good for you in the big scheme of things. But this is not the main point of this chapter. What I'm talking about is when you completely live your life according to other people's expectations. When you make every decision regarding your job, where you'll live and how you'll live your life according to what you think others want out of you. Or more importantly, when you don't do things that you really want to do because they do not conform to what you think other people want you do to.

While you may think you're doing what's right and what is the easiest path for you, it really isn't. This is because you're not living up to your own expectations and when it's all said and done, you'll be much harder on yourself than any of these so-called others are. If you're living a lie, you may be able to fool other people, but you certainly won't be able to fool yourself. What's even more ridiculous about this is that most people really don't care what you do. Or they already know. I know of many people who fretted for years about some secret they held. They were so afraid. But when the secret finally came out, they found out that almost everybody who knew them already knew the secret! Or at least had a suspicion of what the secret was. It was no shock and these people had unnecessarily lived in fear of discovery for years. I know that this is not true for everyone and sometimes, people have good reasons for keeping secrets. This is something that has to be taken up on an individual basis. The point that I'm trying to make is that many times what we're afraid of revealing about ourselves is already out there. We're hiding from no one.

While we fall victim to what we feel are people's high expectations of us, we also can succumb to the low ones as well. I know this certainly happened to me. As I mentioned earlier, while I was always a success in school, I had a very hard time finding a job once I graduated. Seriously, at twenty-one, most of my friends and family looked at me as a total failure. They even said so. "Should have gone to trade school," my parents said repeatedly. "My son certainly won't have all the problems you have," an uncle said. "You might be able to get a job as a janitor. That's the only thing someone like you could do," one of my so-called good friends told me. *And I had only been out of college two months!* Ridiculous. It was like they had been looking for a reason to write me off as a failure. As a result, I began to think of myself as a failure rather than someone who just hadn't gotten started yet. This went on for years until I learned to release. I was very depressed most of the time and blamed myself for all my misteps. This is the same with everybody. Most people who look at themselves as failures just haven't gotten started yet. The main question is whether or not they're happy. And if they are, then maybe they aren't such failures after all.

It's also possible that you maybe have fallen victim to manipulations from malevolent invaduals who want to do harm to you and your character. This can also bring you down just as much. Character assassination is a very real thing and if you're not careful, you'll not only fall victim but also begin to participate in the assassination of your own character. You'll believe the doubts and start to question yourself. You will begin to listen when people are tearing you down. You have to realize that if they're always tearing you down; you may begin to tear yourself down as well. The best thing to do if you're around people who aren't good for you is to not be around them. Believe me, you're much better off being alone than being around people who only want to destroy your self-esteem.

So whatever it is that you're worried about and are trying to conceal or live up to, just let it go. Be happy. Don't let your concerns of other people hold you back. Just release. Just let it go. Your life is your own. Live it. Once you do this and allow yourself the happiness you deserve, the Law of Attraction will really start to happen for you in a good way.

RELEASING

While we briefly touched on the idea of *releasing* in the last chapter in regards to letting other people's attitudes control what you do with your life, there is more to it than that. In fact, it's one of the most important parts of utilizing the Law of Attraction.

As I mentioned earlier, releasing is the idea of letting go. It's the idea of letting God take care of things, if you will. If you're not a religious person, it's the concept of *just being*. You are ready to accept whatever comes. You know that everything happens for a reason. You're not in control of anything. All you can do is your best and hope for the best.

Why this is important in regards to the Law of Attraction is because it is, in essence, the second part of manifesting. Once you manifest, you have to release. In other words, you realize what exactly it is that you want, admit to yourself that you want it and then you release. In other words, you let your manifestation work in the background. You put it out there and then wait for it to happen. You stop thinking about it and enjoy your life. You are prepared for it when it does happen and you are prepared if it doesn't. You know that just because it doesn't happen in the way that you want, it doesn't mean that it isn't going to happen. It just means that either it hasn't happened yet or you aren't quite ready for it.

The concept of releasing can be used in all aspects of your life. Whatever it is that you want or that is bothering you or causing you consternation, you have to do your best and just let it go. You have to go with the flow. No one can control anything and any idea that you can is an illusion or an accident. As I mentioned earlier, if this idea can sink in, you can move on with your life and become a happier person. I know this is a hard thing to do, but once you start it will become easier each time you do it. In fact, you'll begin doing it without even realizing. You will become a much more calm and collected person. You will become happier because you will no longer try to control the universe. Much of the unhappiness of the world comes from the idea that people don't think they are in control of whatever it is they want to be in control of. If they would just realize that this is just a hopeless situation from the beginning, this idea of being in control, then they would be able to let themselves off the hook.

Have you ever noticed how good things always happen to people who are happy go lucky? How they happen for people who just go with the flow? This is because they are releasing. They may not even know what it's called, but they are not sweating and worrying about making things happen. They are letting it happen for them. They are using the Law of Attraction. This is the way you must be. Once you know what you want and just let it go, you'll be amazed at how many opportunities start showing up. Sure, you can white-knuckle it and grit your teeth waiting for your dreams to happen, but is this any way to live? It won't make anything happen any sooner and you'll be miserable while you wait. Dream your dreams and live your life. Good things will happen. Stop worrying and you'll get what you want.

I don't want to sound like I'm oversimplifying the idea of releasing but it really is that simple. If was more complex, it wouldn't work. I know it will be hard to change the way you think, but the next time you really want something to happen, just put it out there and admit to yourself that you want it to happen. Then forget it. Let it work in the background. Don't try to control it. Just do your best at the small portion you can control and then relax. I think you'll be pleasantly surprised at the results.

Releasing is a very simple process. Executing it is not so simple for many people. Especially people who want to be in the driver's seat. However, once you can just understand that this world is so much bigger than yourself and is here for everyone's benefit, maybe you can let go and let the good things happen. Because that's in essence what releasing is. Allowing good things to happen to you. Doesn't everybody want that?

WHAT DO YOU EXPECT?

If there's one thing that you need to take from this book, it's the fact that what you expect out of life is pretty much what you're going to get. For example, if you don't expect that much, you won't be disappointed. You'll probably end up with not that much. This doesn't mean that you have to feel entitled, but rather don't sell yourself short.

In other words, dare to dream. Dare to manifest and go for the gusto. Be responsible in your quests, but never sell yourself short. Always focus on the important things in life. This is the stuff that will either make you happy or advance you in some way. You need to never take your eye from the prize. If you want a bigger house, focus on attaining it. If you're positive, a way will be made apparent to you. If you want a fancier car, don't be afraid to look in the classifieds. One may not be so hard to attain as you might think. Do you want a relationship? Don't ever say that you can't or you're not able to get one. You never know just who you're going to meet. The fact of the matter is that your expectations are what will shape the rest of your life. Sure, some of your expectations may not be met, but wouldn't you rather sometimes have high expectations that aren't met rather than low expectations that always are?

Sometimes, we can't help but have low expectations out of life due to how we were brought up. We turn bad things into good things just so we won't be disappointed. I know that this has certainly happened to me. For example, in my part of the country, it is looked upon as a badge of honor to eat pinto beans and cornbread. It is considered by some to be the "best food you could ever eat." Many people will overlook perfectly delicious food in restaurants in order to order this dish. And many times this is done for the show of displaying just how "down to earth" these people really are. However, the other side of the story is that this is what people used to eat when they had no money. This is what they ate because they couldn't afford anything better. You would think that due to this fact people wouldn't want to be reminded of the poverty that caused them to eat so many beans. But this is not the case. They act—and let me emphasize *act*—like they can't get enough of them. I personally don't care one way or another about them. Because of this indifference, I have always been told by my family members that "you wouldn't have survived back then because that's all we had to eat." Also, I have been told that "you just don't know what it was like or how hard it was." But in the next breath, they will applaud the virtues of the beans and talk about how they just can't get enough of them.

Well, one day I was getting harrassed in this matter when I suddenly realized something. If these people loved beans so much, wouldn't they have been in hog heaven back in the days when they ate nothing else? I suggested this and a deadly silence fell over the room. The subject was dropped and wasn't mentioned again. One person came up to me later and whispered, "I always hated beans."

This is the example that many people have of wanting to live in the past. A nostalgia for the bad times. A person cannot move forward and experience all the Law of Attraction has to offer when they do this. The past is over. The old times are gone. You have to look forward to a bright future, not a dismal past that is being filtered through time.

I know that this is a roundabout way of looking at things, but what these people had done was to make a bad thing into a good thing without really believing it. They were paying homage to something very ordinary and not that great. If you're not careful, this kind of thinking can affect the rest of your life. If you idolize something that was a hardship, you're much more likely to repeat this behavior in the future. When you have options, be glad you have them.

Don't squander them in favor of something like pinto beans. Now, there's nothing wrong with eating beans or anything like that, but it suggests an expectation out of life. If you start thinking that the commonplace and the mundane is acceptable then that is what you're going to get. You can't be bogged down by this kind of thinking. Expect better out of people and relationships and institutions. It's good not to forget your past, but it's not good to keep living like you're still in it.

In order for the Law of Attraction to work, you have to stop thinking that you can't do something or that you don't deserve something. Usually these are just excuses. If you can think it, you can do it. You just have to stop coming up with excuses why you can't. If you're always thinking that you can't do something, it's obviously something you want to do otherwise you wouldn't even be thinking about it. You just have to stop thinking that you can't and just realize you can. You simply need to *really* start wanting it, then your opportunity to do it and a way to do it will be shown to you.

Sometimes people get discouraged because they think something didn't work out for them. They think that life cheated them. But many times, this is really not the case. You get what you expect and many times because a little failure got in your way, you started expecting less. Then you end up with less. When you realize this, you become bitter. But this is not the end of the story. You can always turn this around by expecting more and realizing that every step you have taken to this point has been a learning experience and is simply a place in time before you get what it is that you really want. You just have to be honest with yourself and understand what that is.

I know that's it's easy to get bogged down in the everyday details of life, but you must make an active effort to overcome this. You do this by deemphasizing the petty struggles and distractions that will sidetrack you. You overlook the petty rivalries and things that make you upset.

You stop concentrating on the things that really aren't that important and that you have nothing to gain from. You always think about the positive and what you want out of life.

If you expect the best, you are much more likely to get it. If you expect a happy life, you will be more likely to get it. And if you expect that you're going to succeed, you will. It's only when you don't do this and muddle your mind with distractions and pay homage to bad things as though they are good that you can let yourself be derailed.

Your life is your own. Expect nothing but what you really want.

PLENTY TO GO AROUND

Are you one of those people who think that there's a limited amount of money in the world and that that there's never going to be enough to come your way? Well, if you do, you might as well give up on achieving anything better for yourself because with that attitude, there will never be enough money to go around.

Just because someone else—it doesn't matter who it is—is rich, it doesn't mean that you have to be poor. Keep in mind that a rising tide raises all boats. When someone else is rich, it doesn't only mean that they have more than you, it means that having riches is attainable. It means that you can do it too. You just have to find your way. Everyone is different with different talents.You have to figure out what it is you want and then let the opportunities come to you. And they will come. And they will make themselves known to you.

Money comes and goes. This is just the nature of it. Just as poverty is a condition, so is being rich. But it doesn't have to be bad. Never think that if you're rich in life and in love that you can't be rich in money. This is very foolish and is usually a way people have of consoling themselves because they aren't able to achieve material wealth. You can have it all. You just have to allow yourself to do it. Don't ever think you're expecting too much because you want more out of life.

I know many folks who are some of the most beaten down and broken people you'll ever meet and they will actually look down on people with money. They will scoff at someone who has a new Mercedes and say, "I bet he has more problems than I will ever have." Or they will look at someone with a new house and say, "I don't need it, I'm happy just where I'm at." Or they'll look at a businessman who has failed at his dream and say, "He'd have been better off just throwing his money out the window." To hear them tell it, they are actually superior to people who try to accomplish their goals. In other words, they are better off than successful people because they, themselves, are unsuccessful.

At first, I listened to these people and took them to mean that they were happy with less. That they didn't need nice things or had no desire to accomplish anything. I could relate because this was the way I was brought up. Even so, I thought this was a rather turned around way of looking at things, but each to their own, right? If this is what they thought happiness was, then more power to them. But somehow, something was amiss because they never missed a beat. Anytime someone had more than them, they would never fail to point out some negative aspect of someone else's achievements. Something was definitely not right and the more I listened to people like this, I suddenly realized that they weren't just saying these things to convince me that they were happy with less, they were convincing *themselves*. They were saying these things to convince themselves that they were satisfied without achieving anything they really wanted to do. But the fact of the matter was that they never allowed themselves to achieve the things they wanted because they would never even admit that they wanted them in the first place. To do this would have meant failure to them. They just didn't realize that the difference betweeen people who achieve things and those that don't is the fact that people who achieve things actually make the effort and continue on until they find a way to succeed.

Regardless of how it's presented, jealousy and low self-esteem are big parts of why people think that they can't succeed. People think that they can't succeed because they are somehow inferior to people who do succeed. This is so wrong. Everyone has their niche. They just have to find it.

But first they just have to figure out what that niche is. There is room for everybody and more than enough success to go around.

Regardless of what any negative thinking naysayer tells you, there is plenty for everyone. Sure, the amount of money fluctuates between places and it ebbs and flows, but don't worry that you're not going to get your share. You are. You just have to be positive about it. Money creates more money. There is no limit. More will be printed. More gold will be mined. I'm sure that some gold standard types will argue with me on this, but it's true and there's not much anybody can do about it. Money grows. Wealth grows. Everybody should just try their best to attract their part.

EMPOWER YOURSELF

I know that I've talked about the cycle of debt and how you have to turn it around if you're ever going to experience material wealth. However, there's another thing that's closely associated with the cycle of debt that needs to be discussed if you ever want to be free of it. This is the idea of empowering yourself with your money. Some of you may ask, "Isn't having money empowerment enough?" No, it's not. If you're not careful, your money will rule you rather than empower you. When I refer to empowering yourself, I'm talking about you controlling your money rather than letting it control you.

But how do you empower yourself through your money? It's easy. You give some away. Give and give it freely. You give to charity or others when you can afford it. It's a case of you not having to spend your money only to pay your bills, or to make yourself feel more worthy or important. It's about you giving away money on your own. It will make you feel better and you will attract more good in your life if you do this.

But what if you can't afford it? You can always afford to give a little. Even if it's only some change to the Salvation Army. It will not only make you feel better but will show that you're not completely oblivious to the fact that there are people with even less than you. It will make you appreciative of the fact that you're a fortunate person which will in turn make you even more fortunate because this is a form of manifestation.

There are some people who say that tithing in church is a form of charity and I will agree. If this is where you want your dollars to go, feel free to write that check. Just give.

And give freely. Don't ever begrudge the money either. Keep it flowing and it will flow back to you.

So give a little and empower yourself. Show the universe and yourself that you're in control of your money. Sure, you may have bills but you're more than just a middle man between the person who cuts your paycheck and the company that you pay it out to.

IS GUILT HOLDING YOU BACK?

Are you a responsible person? Are you the type of person who feels that he is truly in control of the world? If this is true, then you're probably also bogged down by a lot of guilt. You probably feel bad over many little things that really aren't that important. In other words, you probably think that you're responsible for much more than you really are. You have to realize that guilt equals control. And if you're a very guilty person who hasn't really done that much to feel guilty about, you probably think you're much more in control than you really are. This is what makes you feel so guilty. This is probably a big part of what is holding you back from truly experiencing what the Law of Attraction has in store for you.

The thing you need to realize is that guilt over stupid things will keep you from getting what you want out of life. By stupid things, I mean situations and events that you cannot possibly have any control over. Times when you did the best you could but it didn't work out as well as it could have. Now of course, there are reasons to feel guilty—especially when you have wronged other people—but in these cases, you must ask forgiveness and do whatever it takes to not feel guilty.

It's amazing just how little we really control in life. Each moment in our lives is fleeting and is gone so fast that we can just hope that we do the right thing. Many times we will but sometimes we won't. It's these times that we need to let go. Sure, you may do things that are really bad, but you should always try to do something to make things right. Apologize and do anything it takes to fix the situation. No one is perfect and you shouldn't think that you are any different. Everyone makes mistakes. Some people just make bigger mistakes than others. The bottom line is that a guilty person is never happy because they always have that cloud hanging over their heads.

People need to assess what they're guilty about and see if it's actually something worth being guilty over. Sometimes you may have legitimate reasons for being guilty. Other times it's just your ego speaking. Are you consumed by guilt over an act you actually committed? Or is it just a technique your mother used to keep you in line and you're still applying this same thinking to yourself? I know that my mother used guilt as a tool. Whenever I did something she didn't like or if there was something she would want me to do, out came the pouting face and the sighs. She would shrug and act as though I had done the worst thing in the world to her by not doing whatever it was that she wanted. She was really bad about this when I was a kid and even worse as an adult. I know this is a ridiculous example but it really happened. I once commented that my wife had bought me some egg nog. Suddenly, the pout came out and then the sighs. I asked her what was wrong. She said, "You said that you didn't like egg nog any more and told me not to buy you any." I had no memory of any such thing and I'm not really sure what her game was, but nevertheless it was just a ploy to make me feel guilty for something. Stories like this abound like this with my mother. However, while this sort of thing used to bog me down when I was younger, once I realized what she was doing, I was free. I began to call her on it. I even began to ask her when she would start, "Are you trying to make me feel guilty for something?" Usually she denies it but I notice that her attempts have gotten fewer and fewer over the years.

The thing to ask yourself is this: Are you assuming a bigger role in the world than what you actually have? Do you feel responsible for things that you don't have anything to do with? The suicide of a friend or family member is a common event that falls into this category. I knew a guy who committed suicide and I know his mother blames me in some way because I didn't visit him regularly. Whenever I see her, she stares blankly at me and refuses to say a word. In her pain, she can't understand that we had drifted apart years before he did it and had virtually no contact for a long time prior. Even so, we were never really that close to begin with. I felt guilt about that for a long time before I was able to rationalize that probably there was nothing anyone could have done to stop him. Suicide was something that ran in his family and he had friends that were much closer to him than I had ever been. I had to realize that while I might have been able to talk to him, I didn't really have that much of an effect on him. I stopped letting my ego do the thinking. It was out of my hands and had I been around him, I know that I would have tried to stop him. However, I wasn't even the same city and we hadn't seen each other in over half a decade.

You have to let yourself off the hook. You're not in control and you don't have as much a sway on the events of the world as some people would lead you to think. All you can do is the best you know how to do at the time. If you can understand this, you will go far.

If you want to attract good things in your life, you have to let this weight of guilt go. Or at the very least, make peace with it. Understand that you did what you could at the time and that if you could have done better, you will do so next time. Or make amends if possible.

This is how you can move on to being a happier person and allowing the Law of Attraction to bring good things into your life.

BAD PEOPLE DO BAD THINGS

Not everyone is a good person and it's completely futile to expect them to be. However, if you're not careful, these people will affect you in ways that you never even imagined. And most of the time it's through no fault of your own.

You may have asked yourself why you're in such a bad condition. Why is it that such bad things always happen to you? You're not a bad person. You do nothing obviously wrong. So why is it that you're stuck in the muck? Are you attracting all this negativity? Why do bad people always seem to single you out for their attention? Are you bringing it on yourself? Is it your fault?

Yes and no.

Yes, you're attracting this, but not because you're "manifesting" bad things. It's because bad people see you as an easy target. You're probably a sensitive person who is nice to others. As a result of this, these people, the ones who prey on nice people, have seen fit to inflict their bad influence on you. While this may seem paranoid and crazy, it's a very real possibility. Has someone ever done something to you that was mean and wrong, yet pretended that either they didn't do it or they apologized immediately, but their explanation didn't make sense? This is your answer. You were targeted.

For example, have you made a date with friends to go somewhere like a concert or a show and it's something that you really wanted to do and talked about it constantly? You arranged the gathering, set the time and the meeting place but the friend who you trusted to pass along information to other friends either "forgot" or got it wrong? You know that there was no real reason for this, but he/she apologized and you got over it. However, if you take a closer look and find that this sort of thing always happens with this particular "friend" then you may be onto something. You'll probably note that this friend is always caught in lies and half truths which are laughed off because he/she's so comical and inept. But really this is not the case. The reason you laugh them off is because the truth is too hard to comprehend. This "friend" may not really be a friend but rather someone who is playing games with your good nature.

Another problem might be that you don't have that many problems at all. It may just be the people around you who have the problems. Maybe they're sabotaging you. Maybe they put you down. Maybe they cause you to have a negative attitude. While it's true that every person is his own boss, sometimes it's just very hard to keep a good attitude when there's always someone throwing crap in your way. This is truly a case when you have to realize that it's not you, it's them.

However, after you decide this is the case and you make the steps to free yourself of the baggage these people are causing you to carry, if you still can't put it together, then you need to possibly rethink things and ask yourself if maybe you're being affected by these people who are *no longer* in your life. If no matter what you do, you still can't break free from these stumbling blocks, then it becomes of a case of it no longer being them, but rather a case of it being you who is the problem. If this is the situation that applies to you, you have to come to grips with what happened to you and move on. Life is too short to let bad people permanently affect how you live your life and view the world.

Of course you're in control of yourself, but sometimes these fake friends will really mess you up in life and most of the time you will never even know what hit you. Choose your friends wisely and know when someone out there is not exactly who they're presenting themselves to be.

One reason many people have problems with self-help and with the power of having a positive attitude is that a lot of the time these sorts of books do not deal with the difficulties that malicious people cause in other people's lives. Many times they simply put the blame on the victim— like they attracted the problem or something. Like the person brought it on himself. I don't believe this. I believe that having a positive attitude and being happy works toward attracting success. However, there are people who I like to refer to as "interlopers." They see good things happening to good people and seek to ruin it. Are they sociopaths? Are they miserable people? Are they jealous? Or are they just mean? It doesn't really matter what their motivations are. What matters is that you know they exist and the only way to cope with them is to keep being positive. Don't blame yourself. Just keep going. Don't change. Eventually, they'll either give up when they can't break you or they'll get bored and move on to the next victim. Retaliating against them will only work some of the time. The reason why is that many times these people think that you are a victim and they will not let themselves be victimized by you. That's why when you strike back they just come back harder. The only way that you can take this approach is to completely hammer back and destroy them the first time. Otherwise, you're just setting yourself up for more of the same. And how do you do this? You become more successful. You attract more wealth. You have an even better attitude. You ignore them. By doing this, you're letting them know that their efforts are weak and that you're much stronger than them. You're letting them know that you are too good to be bothered with trifling issues like someone else's petty jealousies or whatever else is motivating them.

The best defense is to keep going on and being positive because the primary goal of these people is usually to bring you down and make you act like less than you really are. It's very easy to go this route when you're attacked, but avoiding it is your best long term strategy if you want to be a happy person and attract good things into your life. Bad people will do bad things. However, you don't have to keep letting their actions make waves in your life. The best way to win against bad people is to be successful. This is something that they will never be able to handle.

DON'T LET THE BAD STUFF CHANGE YOU

Many people who are down and out and depressed about their lives can look to one event that changed them. They will say that they became a miserable person when their wife left them or when they were robbed of their high school football championship, or whatever.

Don't be this person.

As I said earlier, your life is your own. You have to keep it your own. When you let an event change you for the worse, you are letting it change who you really are. I know that bad things will happen. They happen to everyone, but you have to stay positive. You have to stay true to the real you if you want to attract good things.

I know that there are life-changing events, but everything bad that happens shouldn't become them. I know that you will be hurt when loved ones pass away, but you owe it to their memory to remain being the person that they knew. You owe it to them to become a better person. You owe it to them to remain being the person that they loved and were proud of.

Don't let your emotions own you. Don't look for an excuse to be bad. Stay true to yourself regardless. You'll not only be a stronger person, but you'll also be happier and more successful.

YOU HAVE TO BE HAPPY

One thing that many people who teach about the Law of Attraction overlook is the concept of happiness. They take it for granted that people who are trying to use the Law of Attraction are very happy people. However, this is not always the case. Many people are truly unhappy. This doesn't mean that they don't want to do better. It just means that they feel powerless in their lives and they are at a loss as to how to make themselves feel better. I think that this is the stumbling block that keeps the Law of Attraction from working for them. They just can't get their minds right and as long as they are miserable, there is no way that they will be hopeful enough to manifest or be loosened up enough to release. Happiness is key to utilizing the Law of Attraction. There truly is power in a positive attitude and being happy is the best way to achieve this.

But how can you be happy?

I know it's hard, but it can be learned. But first, you have to realize that it's simply more difficult for some people to be happy than it is others. This is largely because some people are simply happier than others. Why this is the case is anybody's guess, but I've found that happier people are usually better at going with the flow. They don't worry as much because they know there's no point. Everything will work out. Others just can't go along with this. This is because some people just can't let go. They just can't understand that they cannot control the universe and make themselves miserable trying to do so. Happiness equals hopefulness and this is an extremely important concept to recognize. Have you read a classic novel that wasn't hopeful in some way? Even if it is in a nonobvious way? How about a classic movie? There's a reason for this. If it wasn't hopeful, no one would have watched it and it wouldn't have become a classic. This is a universal. This is why you should always be hopeful and happy. Because nothing good will happen otherwise.

You also have to understand that the biggest rule of being happy is that no one can make you happy. Sure some people can make you feel better about yourself but no one can really make you happy. This has to come from within.

So what is it that makes people truly happy? Long term? Money? No. Fame? No. Feeling that you matter? Yes, but there's more. You have to feel loved. I know this is easier said than done, but overall the basic fundamental of being happy is that you must feel loved even it it's only by yourself. You have to feel that you are worthy. You have to feel that your existence does matter in this world. I know this is difficult but once you start feeling loved, the Law of Attraction will begin working and you *will be* loved. People love happy people. This is a basic. And once you start becoming happy, people will be drawn to you. If you have to fake it until you make it and then do it, but remember if you act like you're happy long enough, eventually, you will be happy. You also must be happy in yourself. You just have to accept yourself—you have to release any bad feelings about yourself and your guilt. This will improve your life.

I know that many people out there are lonely and this is why they are unhappy. Loneliness is one of the biggest obstacles to being happy and it is the enemy to almost all people. This is why it is important to overcome it. If you are lonely, it is imperative that you start getting out. It is important that you start involving yourself in activities where you have to be around other people. Sure, you might not like some of the people with whom you will interact, but you must socialize. Once you start to become a social person, you will be come more sociable. This will lead to you meeting more people. You will become happy and then you will start attracting good things into your life. And your happiness will gain momentum.

This leads us to something important. Why is it so important to be happy? It's like this—the Law of Attraction is fueled by happiness. Happiness feeds on itself. You must have a contented mind and must be happy in order for the Law of Attraction to work. Whatever it is you do that you know deep in your heart that you enjoy, you must be happy with it. You mustn't feel guilty. You must accept it and be happy in it. If you can do this, you will attract good things into your life.

I hate to say it, but sometimes I look at awful yet ultra-successful people and wonder how can these people be so fortunate and still be such terrible people. You wonder, how can good things happen to such bad people? Don't they attract bad stuff? The answer is in their happiness. They attract good stuff to them because they are happy in their meanness. Yes, you read right. Being mean makes them happy. This is why good things happen to bad people. This is why you have to take this same principle to heart except do it as a good person. Because when you're doing good things and you're happy and accept yourself, it will not only be that much easier to be happy, but the happiness you spread will multiply.

I know that it will be tough to be happy all the time. You will experience heartbreak and disppointment. If you live life, there is no way around experiencing these situations. You should accept them, but then you have to move on. You have to make the decision whether or not you're going to change who you are and what you believe in because of a disappointment or are you going to go back to who you really are. Are you going to let it make you into a stronger wiser person or are you going to let it turn you into mush? This is something you really need to think about.

Here's an exercise. Take a look around you and see what you have to be happy about. Many of the things you take for granted are things that other people would love to have. Do you have good health? This is something to be happy about. Do you have a loving family? This is something else. Whatever you have and is good, it is something to be happy about. This is how you can find joy and everybody knows that joy is where you find it.

If you're going to be happy, you have to take joy where you can find it. As long as it's not hurting anyone or breaking any laws and you enjoy it, do it. How else are you going to be happy if you don't do the things that make you happy? If you want to attract happiness, you have to be happy yourself.

HARD LUCK, HARD TIMES

Have you ever been around people who do nothing but complain about their finances? No matter what happens, they never have enough money. If they won the lottery, they would complain about the taxes and gripe that it still wasn't enough. In other words, these people are all about hard luck and hard times. Even if it doesn't really apply to them.

I know that hard luck and hard times exist for many people out there today, but you have to realize is that if you want the Law of Attraction to work for you, you can't go around talking about how bad you have it. If you always talk about how broke you are, you will always be broke. You will perpetuate the state of hard luck and hard times just by talking about it. You have to realize that it is mainly a state of mind and if you can turn it around and be positive you will find that positive things will happen for your finances. I know there will be times when you won't have enough money, but you have to work through them and move on to the better times. Instead of talking about how little money you have right now, you have to talk about how much money you will have soon.

In addition to this, no one wants to hear anyone talk about how broke they are. It makes people uncomfortable. And other people who are hard luck and hard times-minded will start getting nervous that you are going to ask them for money.

I know of a woman who does nothing but worry about her money. While she is not hurting for anything, she is always talking about how hard up against it she is. Then one day, she came into a sizable windfall of money. Do you think she stopped talking about how hard up she was? No, not at all. She was then *even more* hard up against it. She began to worry that the windfall wasn't going to be enough to pay her bills. That it wasn't going to last. I can't speak for her, but she didn't seem to appreciate the windfall. She didn't look at it like her prayers were answered, but rather that she now had more money to run out of. Once, when she was complaining about being broke, I told her that I would hate to think how broke she would be if she hadn't come into all that money.

So as you can see, if you worry about money, you won't ever stop worrying. Hard luck and hard times is a state of mind and separates successful people from unsuccessful people Successful people never worry about the money because even when they are broke they know that more is coming. They are confident that the universe or God will provide. This is the way you need to do. Just realize that hard times will pass. They are only a bridge to get you through to the good times.

THE LAW OF ATTRACTION IS WAITING

As I have hoped to explain, the Law of Attraction is an amazingly simple concept. Even so, it is hard to grasp because of the fact that it is so uncomplicated. Perhaps the complication lies in the idea of releasing and letting go and allowing yourself to dream. As children, most of us are encouraged to dream and aspire towards greatness but as we get older we are told that we should stop dreaming and get serious about the world. This is where most people have trouble. They have to unlearn all the things that they have been recently taught and relearn the things that they learned as children. As I have mentioned before, you don't need a system. You don't need to hand over a lot of money to someone to teach you hidden truths and subject you to who knows what else in order to receive the keys to the kingdom. The answers are all within you. You just have to be more positive and open your eyes to what you want.

Above all else, if I can bring one thing home to you in your quest to use the Law of Attraction, it is this: In order for it to work to its full extent, you have to understand that you are worthy. You are worthy of everything you hope for. You are worthy of everything you work for. Most importantly, you are worthy of everything you receive. It doesn't matter what your history is or what you've done. If you can fix your attitude and start being positive, positive things will happen. Your self-esteem is crucial. You have to know that you're good enough. You have to feel that you belong anywhere you go. This is what the Law of Attraction is about: Attraction. And once you feel that you're worthy of all the good things the world has to offer, you will be ready to start receive them.

The Law of Attraction is waiting for you to use it. Aren't you ready to let it?